Of **SOULS** *and* **SNOWFLAKES**

an Adoption Story

by TIFFANY CHILDS

Xulon
PRESS

www.xulonpress.com

DEDICATION

To Micah, my safe place -- Wherever you go, I go. Also to Andrew, Elijah, Isaac, Eliana, and Isabella, who remind me to dance and play. I am so proud of you and am so glad to be your mommy.

ACKNOWLEDGEMENTS

This book would not be possible without the love and support of my husband. Micah, you have been privy to the spontaneous expelling of loads of information (sometimes coherent, sometimes not) and frequent, impassioned outbursts of emotion for many years. You have been faithful, my sweetheart. There were conversations you and I shared over many long, uncertain nights that gently nudged me toward the Good News both in word and deed. I was never alone in coping with such deep, painful revelations. You always listened and many times encouraged with truths that are unchanging. More than anything, you have suffered, laughed, and everything in between with me. You are indeed my most trusted companion and one true love in this life.

Thanks to my mom, who has been my biggest cheerleader for as long as I can remember. Thank you for your willingness to edit even the wordiest of chapters and blog posts. Your enthusiasm for grammar is a most welcomed help.

Thanks to Eric Johnson, who was the first person to tell me I was a perfect mother in Jesus. I will never forget this first time God allowed me to wonder at the Gospel as an adult, no holds barred. You have been instrumental ever since. Also to his bride, Becky, who has carried deep hurt with me in an authentic way. I am so thankful for and will always remember the way you physically wept with me.

Thanks to my girl friends all along the way, who have journeyed with me through both pain and joy. I know I am a pretty heavy friend to carry sometimes! You all have helped shape me in ways God was so kind to orchestrate. I love you all dearly. I am thankful for those of you who have even read and been kind enough to help in editing this book! Having these words in your hands first has been a comfort. Thank you for all your encouragement.

Thanks to those who helped move me toward publishing in different ways; I am so appreciative.

Thanks to the members of LaGrange Baptist Church, who paralleled this season of life with my family and me. We will not soon forget the practical kindness given to us (or all the diapers!). To Pastor Tony who, in and through suffering, allowed me to be sad, solemn, and even questioning without showing alarm. Not all pastors possess this kind of ability to care for a fragile soul. Thank you and Joie for your friendship.

Thanks to all my family, thank you for your love, sweet support, and prayers. You all have been instrumental in my life and I am thankful for each one of you.

Thanks to those who preach the Gospel without apology week in and week out, as well as those who speak and write about it freely. When I need reminding there is Good News, I know where to go. This includes my current church home, St. Francis in the Fields, Louisville, Kentucky. Jady, Nick, and Bob (and their wives) are the kindest souls. May God continue to bless you as you serve His church.

Endorsements

"Mothers are ordinary heroes, whose mighty deeds are usually masked by their mundanity. What makes this maternal story special is the weaving together of technological miracles with the miracle of a heart opening up to greater grace, by means of great tragedy and personal limitations."

Eric L. Johnson

Professor of Pastoral Care, The Southern Baptist Theological Seminary

"With Of Souls and Snowflakes, Tiffany Childs has given a thoughtful, personal, and inspirational account of a family's desire for children that dramatically illuminates the intersection of the Gospel with the modern world. Situated within the contemporary world of cutting-edge reproductive medical technology, her story is nevertheless an age-old account of how amid the stresses and desires for children, the enduring message of the Gospel remains not only the hope that sustains in the midst of suffering and loss, but also gives the framework for human existence itself. Hers is a story about how the promises of God for his people are the foundation for the house that not only stands firm in the midst of the wind and waves of life, but gives its inhabitants the radical confidence to stand on the rooftop, singing his praises."

John D. Koch, Jr.

Rector, St. Francis in the Fields, Louisville, KY

"This is a tremendous story! In this book, Tiffany Childs tells this moving account of her embryo adoption with a refreshing vulnerability and transparency that draws you in and keeps you. She invites the reader into some deep, dark places of her hurting soul and brings gospel truth and clarity that is both comforting and inspiring. She also forces a largely ignored, but needed conversation about the reality of thousands of frozen embryos that are left in the shadows. Anyone

who has lost a child, or struggles with infertility will find a path to healing and hope through this remarkable story. I highly recommend it."

Brian Croft

Senior Pastor, Auburndale Baptist Church, Louisville, KY

Founder, Practical Shepherding

Senior Fellow, Church Revitalization Center, The Southern Baptist Theological Seminary

"*Tiffany's story is one of suffering, pain and redemption. It is a story about uncovering law and discovering grace. About death and new life. In exposing her own wounds to us we are invited to enter in and explore ours. This book welcomes us into a part of Tiffany's soul and the work God is doing in the midst of pain and suffering. Though I have not personally struggled with infertility, Tiffany's messages of self-imposed law and undeserved grace minister to my heart and soul like water in a parched land. Whether you are someone who suffers with infertility, you are walking alongside someone who is suffering with infertility, or simply are a person who is suffering, I recommend to you this book, if for no other reason than to see the suffering of someone who is able to say "I believe, Lord, help my unbelief".*

Cara Croft, Pastor's Wife, Auburndale Baptist Church, Louisville, KY

Co-author, The Pastor's Family

"*Tiffany Childs has written a beautiful account of her family's journey to adopt "snowflake babies." The author writes with such eloquence and honesty that I felt as if I was reading her heart being poured out on every page. Her story communicates a much bigger truth for all of us, the deep love of our Heavenly Father for His adopted sons and daughters. Everyone, whether considering adoption or not, will be blessed by reading this book.*"

Jaime Wolter, Pastor's Wife, Oakhill Church, Humboldt, IA

PREFACE

T his is a story about the God of Universe and His love for this broken, sinful girl. Most specifically, it is the story He has been writing in my life and the lives of the others in my family and how it bears witness to such love. With that in mind, it also serves as a record. There are times in the Bible when God says to take care "lest you forget," and in part these words are a stack of stones built high to remember the works of the Lord. There is something to be shared here, and in this far from perfect way, I want to share it.

I have always been fascinated by stories, especially the stories of those God chooses to include in the Book He gives us to know more of Him. The people involved are always flawed and fallen, but their lives are linked together in a holy history that points to the One who unifies them. In the end, the stories are not really about the people involved, but say more about God Himself. I am in the company of those loved by God throughout the ages. My desire is to add my voice to those who have seen a great Light. Thankfully, God still redeems all kinds of sinners and as He moves though time, grace is continually proven amazing.

Miraculous things are happening all around us. There are extraordinary things that happen in the lives of ordinary people. As compelling as one story may be, there is always context that brings about layers of discovery and awareness. There are stories we hear that seem to be about one thing, but as I want to remember, in every one thing I may see there are a thousand more things God is doing[1]. I do not claim to know all those things, but in the wake of Love and Divine Providence, I wish to know more of every good thing, to the praise of the One who ordains and saves.

~

These all died in faith, not having received the things promised, but having seen them and greeted them from afar, and having acknowledged that they were strangers and exiles on earth. For people who speak thus make it clear that they are seeking a homeland. If they had been thinking of that land from which they had gone out, they would have had opportunity to return. But as it is, they desire a better country, that is, a heavenly one. Therefore God is not ashamed to be called their God, for He has prepared for them a city.
Hebrews 11:13-15

I in no way am comparing my life to the lives of Abraham, Sarah, Isaac, or Jacob. I just think for sure they had mundane moments — Sarah sweeping out the tent or preparing another meal or Abraham, mending his sandals or carrying his sons on his shoulders — just like in my experience. I am grateful that my unconsciousness does not affect eternal outcome in the slightest and that God is always conscious of all things and working toward our ultimate realization of His glory.

A more contemporary way of expressing this same realization I found in a Christine Dente song:

---

[1] John Piper, "Piper: "God is always doing 10,000 things in your life, and you may be aware of 3 of them," https://twitter.com/desiringgod/status/266584993881550849 (Nov. 8, 2012).

So I listen in and I hear the song
From another country and I sing along
And I play my part as the story goes
And the difference that it will make is yet to be told

All my life
Is an answer to the invitation?
To be a part of the conversation
Living in a bigger story
All this time
Is history-in-the-making
Always headed for a destination
To take my place in a bigger story[2]

On March 31, 2009, I entered this into our online family journal, Joy in Our Journey[3]. I have included other excerpts along the way.

---

[2] Christine Dente, "Bigger Story," by Christine Dente, Scott Dente, and Charlie Peacock, *Becoming* (Rocketown Records. 2003).

[3] www.joyinourjourney.blogspot.com

CHAPTER 1

I was not unlike most girls in their teens, measuring the future in the light of the present — ready for independence and ready to grow up. I may have been ready to grow up a bit more quickly than others, though. The phrase, "Too big for my britches," comes to mind. Sometimes it serves me well. God is kind to give tenacity to those who will need it.

After a string of boyfriends (or whatever one might call persons of the opposite sex with whom I had interest but was not allowed to date) at the tender age of fourteen, I asked God to bring me a future husband. The reason it is so memorable is that I wrote it down. I have always been an easily distracted person and writing prayers seems to give me a connectedness to words that soul-speaking lacks. I remember clearly having sadness over past relationship decisions (if you can call what I had "relationships" with such inexperience) and realized I was headed down a dangerous path. God is always so kind to instill in this believer the weight of the law, appropriate to my development. It was and is a gift. My prayer was in response to much reflection and born out of repentance, but it was also a "waving the white flag" moment. I am also dramatic. I guess you could say that came a bit early in my dating career but as I reflect back on those days, cutting to the chase is part of my giftedness and cursedness.

I remember saying something like, "Dear God, I am really tired of all these boys. Please just send me the one I am to marry and I will."

Just three days later, on a brisk January evening (the fifteenth to be exact), my eyes met those of my future husband in the living room of his parents' home right before a youth rally. A mutual friend had decided we should be introduced. There are two things I remember most from that night. First, I had to wear my mother's coat and was sure that I would be judged seriously uncool. Second, and most emotionally illicit, I remember the way a most handsome young man sauntered into his living room and glanced at me for the very first time. From the minute I met Micah, I knew he was the one God had designed to be my lifelong companion. The way he lifted his hands during "Cast your Burdens" (also known as the "High-ya High-ya" song) sealed the deal. I even told my mother when I arrived home from the event, partly in jest, that I was going to marry him someday. Four years later, I did.

For those of you reading who are still waiting on the one whom you will share this life, I have no idea why God chose to answer so clearly and so quickly. I do know for me it was grace clearly demonstrated to a wandering heart. There are no prescriptions here of, "Look at me and my faithfulness." The only thing I have to say about the way all that went down is, "Look at God and His faithfulness."

The two of us were very young, eighteen and nineteen years old, when we married. I had not even begun to have mature thoughts about God and His providential plans for those He loves. When Micah and I sat down to talk through our thoughts about what he and I desired for our family, we answered all the typical questions with him and me at the center of the universe: where we would live, our hopes and dreams for the future, our expectations of marriage, etc. What we really wanted the most out of the whole thing was to be together all the time. I just did not want to leave him — ever. It did not matter that we were freshmen in college and that no one else around us was married. Whatever it took to make it work, we were willing to do it. The one pre-marital question, however, that was most important to me was our plans for children. We both wanted a big family. With that checked off the list, we moved ignorant of ignorance, headstrong and hopeful into our future.

It is funny to me now. Lack of life experience combined with a false sense of control shaped our answers to those questions. Maybe the way the questions were phrased was partially to blame. I do remember thinking that if we chose four children as an ideal number, we would have them eventually. I understand the reasoning for the question. I know it is important to make sure couples are not surprised with major disagreements about family size, but I was naïve and narcissistic. Those two things in combination are no good for anyone. I am not sure how receptive I would have been then to the truth that God is the Creator and Sustainer of all things and its implications for conception.

When it was all fleshed out, we both loved children, wanted children, and we thought it would be a good thing if we could add to our family through biological means as well as through adoption. While we both had ethical and spiritual reasons for wanting to adopt, it was not really more than a simple desire in the beginning. I did not think I would ever not have genetic children and adopted children, nonetheless.

The honeymoon did not last very long, and neither did our self-assuredness of the answers on our pre-marital questionnaire. After just a few months of marriage, I was diagnosed with endometriosis. I had my first surgery to treat the disease at age nineteen. Both Micah and I wondered if our desires for a large family would be in God's plan for us. I remember a time when Micah looked tenderly at me and reassured me of his affection with or without the addition of children to our family. He was loving and kind, but hearing the words out loud ripped my soul open in front of my new husband. I did not want to have to entertain the possibility.

I am one of the "old-fashioned" ones. I have always known in the depth of my being that I wanted to be a mother. Micah and I had received some well-intentioned advice as newlyweds to wait a while to consider having children. To this day, while I am sure this advice could serve some couples, I must be careful in assuming that I can measure the future for anyone. We should know better, as one in eight couples experiences some type of difficulty in conception. Even though I was not sure if that was the most wise following my diagnosis, we were in agreement and compliant. There were pressures in working and attending school that made it unwise for us to bring a baby into our family. Still, not being able to have children had been a fear from the day the abbreviation "endo" was introduced into my vocabulary. The bottom line: God gives most women, especially this one, the desire to mother. While I was uncertain of the timing, I was all in. Having that desire so palpable in my soul was something God would use (and continues to use) to show me some very clear things about who He is and who I am. It would be the beginning of a most important lesson in His Fatherhood of rebellious persons in a profound and inescapable way.

In those first years of marriage, a melancholy music began to play in the quiet recesses of my unsteady soul and I began a most vulnerable dance with my Author Father that would bring great joy and great pain.

CHAPTER 2

After two and a half years of a crash course in we-are-young-newly-married-and-away-from-our-birth-families, Micah and I moved to Louisville, KY where he began as a student at Boyce College. It was not long before I met other student wives and was astounded at the budding, blooming, and constantly growing families all around. Everyone either had children or children on the way, or at least that is how it seemed at the time. One person I met early on through a student wives' seminar was a gentleman who was both a retired OB/GYN and Professor in Pastoral Counseling and spoke to the student wives about women's health and fertility issues. I had already had both a laparoscopy and lumpectomy by this time and when I found myself personally fitting his program profiles at a particular event, I waited around afterward to speak with him. Dr. Bill Cutrer kindly and graciously took time to answer the questions about my prognosis within a few minutes. I was struck by his compassionate, knowledgeable manner.

I left having never seriously considered Micah's and my choices and their effect on my fertility and his words weighed on me in a momentous way. It made me question our choosing to wait on making childbearing a priority, especially given my previous diagnosis. I had always taken other advice about waiting a while and thought especially since we had married so early, I would not have to even think about timing. When I returned home, Micah was open, understanding, and willing to rethink where we were in space and time. One thing is true: When couples decide it is time to start having babies, their part is only in cooperation with the will of the Creator. I would get a lesson in this I would not have willingly signed up for in any other context.

We began the prayer, "God, please add to our family." There has been a definition of prayer that has stuck with me through many years. When I pray, it is more than voicing requests, praise, or repentance, but an exercise in aligning my will to my Father's. As I prayed, I always felt that God's will was to increase our family. His will felt more like, "This is good and right but indeed mysterious, and I know you have no idea of my plans for you, but press on." I know this aligning of perceived wills sounds subjective, but I had no truths that stood in opposition. I prayed often for Him to help me through this process, whatever it may be.

Moving forward in recognizing the effects of my disease and acknowledging a need to be vulnerable to God's will in childbearing was the easiest part of adding to our family. It is a story that is not too uncommon. As days turned to weeks and weeks into months of failed attempts, I began to come to grips with the fact that this would not be an easy road for Micah or me. Surrounded by women at the same point in life as me yet getting pregnant constantly, I was in agony. There were reminders of Micah's and my inability to conceive all around me. While I would not dare admit it then, I felt like God was mocking me. I would simultaneously be in physical pain from endometriosis in addition to mental anguish of infertility and be invited to a function where we were the only childless couple. Once I was at a party where Micah and I were the only family of two and upon that realization, I was unable to function. Honestly, my response was surprising to me. I did not wake up that morning desiring to make myself an outcast. I did not know what to do with those feelings that were clearly not showing satisfaction and contentment in my present circumstances. Nevertheless, truth be known, I wanted to connect with the ladies and their talks about diapers and beginning solid foods.

There was a not-so-secret group of women who shared in their struggles to conceive hosted by Dr. Cutrer. He was a valued resource at the meetings held in the quiet of the evenings on the seminary campus. Here was a place where children were valued, encouraged, and mandated as a God-given result of a God-honoring marriage, yet there I sat among those who just could not conceive. Our bodies (or our husbands') would not allow it. I was so thankful for the women who were compassionate toward me and gave me a place to fit in for a while. The meetings provided an atmosphere of pain and hope. The gal who facilitated the meetings always expressed her desire that each one of us would "graduate" from the group. I was burdened with the thought that I should be okay even if I did not. Well, of course I should.

On the same campus, there were the voices of others; particularly the voice of the idolatry-warners. It was not difficult for me to agree that my heart is indeed an idol-factory. At one event I remember very well, there was a section in the speakers' presentation directed at women dealing with infertility. The speaker made it clear that if a woman attends what he called a support/self-pity group for the expressed interest of coping with childlessness, she was an idolater. This meant she desired children more than she desired God's plan for her. She desired children more than she desired God. She would sin to have children or sin if she did not have children. This was the same space where I had found comfort in the company of women who shared in my struggles. I was not sure how to reconcile the messages.

I went home, read the account of Hannah and how the priest thought she was intoxicated because of her verbal, open desire for a child. I wondered what the speaker might do with her. While her story was an encouragement, I would then face warnings about covetousness and misplaced love as I looked at her promise fulfilled in giving Samuel back to the Lord. That part of the story was difficult for me.

I would be reminded in a different circumstance that I do not have because I do not ask. It was all very confusing and it left me in a no-win situation. I did not know how to pray. I would constantly find myself mid-prayer, afraid of praying too much, therefore admitting my idolatry, or not enough and lax in my faith in the God Who gives all things. My childlessness seemed for a time completely reciprocal. If I do and say the right things, God will bless me. If I do not, He will not. I knew my lack of trust in God in childlessness was part of some faith equation. I have to just say right now — That is the farthest thing from the gospel, but it was what I felt I was hearing over and over as the days and months dragged on. Through it all, I always fell on the side of asking. It always was the thing I was called to do. I have always been one to succeed and I just would not, could not give up. It is a blessing and a curse, my friends.

In the fall of 2002 and after months and months of negative pregnancy tests, things began to get a little more precarious. Micah was out of town on a weekend retreat and I was home alone. I had some abnormal bleeding and was beginning to get concerned. I called the physician on call at my OB/GYN office and relayed my symptoms. The doctor requested that I do a home pregnancy test. It never occurred to me that might be a possibility.

The test was positive.

I called my husband as he was on the road returning from his trip with the news. It was bittersweet. Naivety is sometimes a blessing. I do believe that while I felt concerned, I was genuinely excited. There were two lines on a pregnancy test. In the abundance of negative ones, I had never seen that before! It is true that plans for that child began as quickly as the words, "I am pregnant," left my lips. The bleeding did not subside and Micah and I quickly learned that the little one who had been with us had left just as quickly as he or she came.

For those who have walked Hannah's road, miscarriage can be a blow in the most disconcerting way, reinforcing the battle of anxieties. On top of everything, I had a doctor who personified the callousness to the statistic that as many as one in three conceptions end in miscarriage. She did not seem to care that I had prayed for many months for a child, God had given me my request, but only for a very short time. I was crushed. Even in the loss of my first child, I had become what I so desired to be; a mother. Even so I would not, will not, meet this child for a very long time.

There is something very godly and beautiful in a woman's cry for children. I only recently realized why it makes logical sense that it is so near to a female soul to carry and nurture a child. In the garden, God clearly directs Adam and Eve to bear children. While I do not believe this mandate can be applied to everyone across the board, as God has different callings for different people, it is another thing at which we as cursed human beings fail.

I remember so clearly my dear doctor/pastor friend speaking at length about the fact that human beings are the worst at procreation of all sexually reproducing beings on the planet. Our body systems reflect our fallen state in this one area so distinctly. As part of the curse, the same phrase seems to be repeated in Genesis 3: "I will surely multiply your pain in childbearing; in pain you shall bring forth children." There are some commentators that agree that the implications of sin do not end in the physical birthing of babies, but in the ability to conceive and even in raising children. For a person with knowledge of what honors God in procreation, that can be heart-wrenching!

After a long process of healing from losing our first baby, I moved through more months of waiting and asking. I also began to hint a bit of displeasure in my soul with a God who had allowed such pain. I was too well versed in Christian-ese at the time to say much more than that, even though I began to doubt that He really loved me at all.

As far as learning to cope with infertility, it was within this season of waiting that I learned something very important: differentiation, or perceiving the differences between others and myself. I did not learn it completely on my own. Like many good lessons, I gleaned from someone else's story. I do not remember who gave such clarity to a mixture of feelings, but it made complete sense and offered me a clear way to cope. I felt it gave me hope in trying to maintain some relationships with other women in varying places in life. I realized, as the scripture says, that life mixes happiness (rejoicing with those who rejoice) and sadness (be simultaneously sad for me). It provided some way to honor my own pain and love my neighbors. I did not always do it well and deep down I knew I felt real struggle, but I wanted to try. I often felt guilty when I was not as happy for others as I should be. Every day was a get-up-and-try-again day.

In the midst of those days, Micah and I had to have the most romantic conversation ever. We had to discuss to what extent we would utilize reproductive technology. I bought a book on the subject from Dr. Cutrer and his colleague Sandra Glahn. After reading, thinking, and praying, he and I privately came to the conclusion that treating my endometriosis was one thing, but making use of much more was beyond our comfort level. This discussion would continue as we navigated through different medical interventions. Inviting a doctor into our bedroom was difficult. Just saying certain things out loud can be difficult enough as it openly admits the problem. Saying those things out loud to someone I hardly knew at the time and giving intimate details was even more rattling.

Eventually, I made an appointment with my OB/GYN and soberly mentioned our struggles. The good thing about my doc at the time was that he had a very mild bedside manner. I needed that quality in a physician since I tend to freak out sometimes. His suggestion was to use clomid, an ovulation induction medication to help regulate my sporadic cycles and hopefully give more opportunity for conception. His recommendation in a low dose form did not exceed what we felt was appropriate in treating my physical issues.

If you want to kill a marital, physical relationship, well, giving two people an intimacy schedule is one of the ways to do it. These were tough months. It seemed that every day I was medicinally meant to be near my husband, he and I would get into some type of disagreement. Then, conflicts began because of the disagreements. Many things that had been good between us and were even endearing in our relationship were somehow skewed within the struggles we were facing. At the same time for these many months, he and I began to get a glimpse of the amount of commitment we had for each other. We had been through hardships before. This was a new level of intimacy and knowing that would bind us together.

When the first dose of medication did not work for several months, our doc asked us to consider adding a bit more. Prayerfully, we asked God for wisdom in this and did agree. It is difficult to communicate significant portions of time in the written word on a page. Suffice it to say it was an entire season of adjusting and waiting.

Not too long ago, Micah said one of the most loving things I have ever heard. He simply stated that there are things only he and I know, have experienced, and share together. That seems oddly obvious, but that acknowledgement and the intent behind the words — that he loves me while knowing so much of me, good, bad, and seriously ugly, and does not reject me — is love lived. Of course Micah does not do it perfectly, but going through months and months of infertility solidified his intention to stay in difficult circumstances.

CHAPTER 3

The morning I found out I was pregnant with Andrew, I woke up early and took a home pregnancy test before I had to head to work. I hardly slept the night before. I remember slipping into the bathroom and having about a minute to myself before shouting it to the rest of the world. I was so excited and Micah was sleeping. It was all I could do to abstain from jumping up and down on the bed in a full-blown freak-out (I warned you) to awaken him with the news. I did finally plant myself beside him and tried to play it cool with an, "I'm pregnant!" Funny how news of this sort quickly wakes a guy up. I called my mom. I told my friend Kristi downstairs, who rejoiced with us. She was a good friend who shared in our excitement and took a picture of me standing in her doorway to make a memorial of the moment. I went to work beaming. I felt as though it was written all over my face as I walked into the office. I was sure they would all know, but was elated when I could say it aloud. I told another dear friend, Cara, later in the day and she practically dislocated my arm, sharing in our excitement.

The next months were spent in preparation for this little life that would be joining us out in the world. These months were the beginning of what I affectionately refer to as "Delusion Land." I honestly thought that if I read enough, had enough outside input from other mothers, and prayed enough, I would do absolutely everything right with my firstborn. Those thoughts were banished almost immediately upon Andrew's arrival.

Andrew was born five weeks before his due date. The birth itself took us so off guard. One minute I was sitting at a progress appointment and the next, I was being wheeled past laboring women (who in my estimation were about to self-combust), trying to understand why I was jumping in front of them. Two hours later, I would know why. I was very glad for those short hours. It gave time for a neighbor to bring us our camera. Needless to say, we were ill prepared.

After all my experiences of praying for this sweet child, my first minutes of seeing the face of flesh and blood called by name — my husband's and my name — was deeply moving. I had heard it said a thousand times but it is true; the pain of birth is driven away by the joy of those hands, those eyes, that skin, that smell. Greeting a soul connected to mine in the warmth of skin-to-skin and nourishment of mother's milk was one of the purest experiences I have had in this life.

Returning home with our Andrew began a whirlwind of first-time-parenting. I recently found a journal entry written a few months after he was born. Hearing myself speak in the past in this way marks my journey to this current place with a lantern of solidarity and connectedness now twelve years into parenting. This confession is the first of many that I categorize in the, "I don't trust God as I should," place. I am glad that in the quiet, God gave me space to begin my journey to honesty.

> *Journal Entry, July 2004 ~ I will never forget the moment a delivery room nurse placed a 5 pound, 13 ounce little boy in my arms 5 weeks before he was due and said, without actually saying, "He's all yours! Now go and make him healthy and gain weight."*

*In my mind I was thinking, "Oh, this will be a piece of cake —
after giving birth to him un-medicated! I surely can do that
along with put him on a schedule, read the Bible to him, dress
him, change him, burp him, hold him and continue to take
care of my home and husband all at the same time." I had
read every book on child-rearing given to me and I knew I
was ready for this responsibility.*

*Call me ambitious, but this is what I had wanted for so long.
I was sure I was ready. My husband and I had prayed for
a child for more than two years before the birth of our son.
Through struggles with infertility and miscarriage, my heart
had grown to love this child before he was ever conceived.
Now, this much-awaited child was lying in my arms, looking
up at me through blurry eyes. This was one of the most precious moments I have had in my life.*

*After a little time in the delivery room for us all to get aqua-
tinted, we were whisked away to begin living together in our
hospital room. That first night, it was all I could do to take
my eyes off of my child long enough to try and sleep, but by
the wee hours of the morning, I was in desperate need for rest.
Much to my frustration, my rest was hindered by an adverse
reaction to pain medication. I remember thinking that one
hour of sleep probably wasn't **all** that I needed to begin motherhood, but **surely** I would catch up.*

*Needless to say, I didn't. Actually, those first two weeks were
the most sleepless I have experienced. There are many things*

I don't remember about those first weeks. The world around me began to fade away. It was suddenly just me, my little one, and the home health nurses who monitored "how we were doing."

I am not exactly sure the moment it happened. It may have been as we were driving home from the hospital, or maybe while we were still there and nurses were explaining that if Andrew didn't nurse they would have to give him a bottle. Maybe it was later at home when I was watching him spend another 2 hour stretch under bili-lights. Perhaps when I had the chance to think back at the nurse's comments I was reminded I was the only one in the world that had all that Andrew needed to live. Whatever "it" was, "it" has been something that has shaken me to the core ever since. If you have ever had a first child, you will understand what I mean. The weight of responsibility of raising a child, and here I mean physically raising him and helping him grow, was overwhelming. I am not even speaking of the responsibility of raising him up in the fear and admonition of the Lord — only the physical aspect.

So I am led to my first struggle of motherhood: the responsibility of keeping another human being alive.

I had heard it said that Andrew is God's and I am only his caretaker. I believed this somewhat, but in those first days, I was sure that if I wasn't close to him, watching his every breath, he would surely die. As his chest rose and fell, my chest rose and fell. If he went longer than a few seconds without steady breathing, I would grab his hand or touch his belly. I fed him every two hours, at the doctor's advice, and watched as he seemed only to lose weight in those first few days. I scrutinized every bump and mark on his little body. As I had been told, I was the one who had been given this responsibility. I could not fail or quit, even if it meant giving up what I needed for my own survival.

There were many sleepless nights, worries, and excuses those first weeks. Why could I not trust God with this baby? There is a verse in Psalms that had helped me through other sleepless nights in my past. I had quoted it many times before, but had not recalled it for some time. Then one evening as I was lying near Andrew in his crib when he was a few weeks old, I whispered to him Psalm 4:8, "I will lie down and sleep in peace, for you alone, O Lord, make me dwell in safety." The words struck me as though I was hearing them for the first time. David, who had many adversaries, had trusted the Lord as he rested. I also remembered God's response to Job in Job 38. I realized that I was implying with my lack of trust that the Lord God, who "gives orders to the morning" and "shows the dawn its place," cannot take care of my child. Then, like a whisper in the wind, I was reminded that it was He, and He alone, that was and is the maker and sustainer of all things. I had to then give Andrew back to the Lord who had given him to me. That night, as I laid Andrew into his crib and into the Lord's arms, I could dwell in safety as I got much needed rest as well. Andrew is the Lord's and the Lord is mine.

I have to remind myself of this truth daily as I wrestle with control. The fact remains that although he is my responsibility, my son ultimately rests in much better hands than mine.

Even while I was in the post-delivery healing stage, I began showing signs that, against all knowledge of how the disease usually operates, my endometriosis had returned. Again, after months of waiting and enduring much pain, I broke down and called my doctor. This time, my OB/GYN sent me to a reproductive endocrinologist. This meeting would change the course of our lives. A very knowledgeable, compassionate, and forward man, he took care of me with great skill. It was a different experience, arriving at his office. It was a place of great pain. The couples there were all struggling. It confirmed to me that I did have a difficult issue. I was glad to have such an informed ally in my new doctor. Upon his recommendation, I was faced with another surgery and another season of minimally invasive reproductive assistance. It was concerning that my endometriosis was so aggressive and I so symptomatic.

On the third of only three months of treatments, I learned of my little Elijah. It was evening and very quiet. I have never been one to hold such grand news to myself, so after telling Micah I called on my friend Cara, once again, to share in my excitement. She was not just any friend, but a friend who had willingly entered into my struggles, sufferings, and pain. I was thankful for the season of solace with her at my side and now, another season of joy.

Even with a two-year-old to care for, my pregnancy with Elijah was smooth and delightful. I am sure that he spent all his days in-utero lounging and reading all the appropriate developmental/behavioral books that made him such an easy baby. I did have some signs of premature labor, but with medication and a few weeks bed rest he arrived the day after my birthday, 2006. In the quiet of a bright, summer Louisville morning, we welcomed our sweet Elijah Haddon into our arms. His big brother loved him, too. At that time, Micah was the pastor of a church outside of Louisville. The loving members helped us welcome him. I remember wanting so much to backtrack and tell them what a miracle this child was to me. I wanted them to know the months and months I had prayed for him.

> *Today I am trying to acclimate myself to this new season of life... trying to figure out how I am going to remain an honorable wife to my husband and raise these precious boys and at the same time not fade into a world of matchbox cars and Clifford the Big Red Dog. I was just speaking to a dear friend this morning about how our minds as moms dull due to sleep deprivation and the constant decision-making staying at home with children demands (ex. PB & J or cheese toast, re-clean the kitchen or pick up the living room again, changing diapers or clothes on someone, which one... or both!). I thought throughout the day about our conversation and about something I had examined before but am especially thankful for on a day like today. Amid life's changing seasons, God is never having to adapt to anything. He is as He has always been. The fact that I don't even have the mind to acknowledge Christ's sacrifice on my behalf doesn't lessen its power to sustain and continually change my life. I am so thankful it doesn't depend on me. That in and of itself is*

holding me up today and giving me hope for tomorrow and the remaining seasons of my life. JIOJ, July 19, 2006

Our lives began as a family of four and one in heaven. Each of our capabilities and strengths better shaped our home into a more diverse and fun place to live. I have loved getting to know my husband day in and day out, as well as my children. There are things about them all that make me laugh and things that make me gasp! We have always had the gift of being very close to each other, both as I have had the honor to stay home and as Micah's center of gravity, earth-side speaking, falls at home as well.

After Elijah was born, Micah and I had learned not to trust any pre-conceived notion about how God may order our family. We did not assume we could choose space between he and any other children we desired to have, and we did desire more. Again, it seemed as if our family was not complete. As quickly as a year after Elijah's birth, I needed yet another surgery for endometriosis. We did another round of medication to try and achieve a normal cycle and pregnancy but at the end of a few months, God did not allow this to happen.

Once again, it is difficult to communicate time in a book like this. It is an element that, in retrospect, can feel unimportant. Yet in living the days, months, and years, it becomes a character in the story. The years of struggle, prayer, and waiting taught me more about the blessing of children than I could have been taught otherwise. Time and suffering were diligent, relentless teachers.

I remember a phone conversation with my friend Cara, discussing the outcome of our final medication trial. In a way, I think she and I had both braced for the sight of a closed door. It was painful. Having these experiences placed Micah and me into a different category of couples. Our diagnosis: Secondary infertility, or the inability to achieve pregnancy after having a genetic child or children. It is a title that is difficult to talk about. I think Sandra Glahn and Dr. Cutrer do a good job of explaining why:

Secondary infertile couples are at an in-between place. The fertile population perceives them as having no fertility problem because they've conceived. Yet whena they are among the infertile population, they feel too ashamed to ask for support for fear childless couples will resent them.[4]

Turning around to see what was behind me, I was very thankful for both of the boys. God had given me two miracles. There are many fears associated with parenting in the light of fertility issues. I have always been concerned that Andrew and Elijah feel they are unique blessings, but gratitude does not replace longing or erase pain. I did not deny the path of pain or continued longing. I did not even deny that God ordained those things. Nevertheless, I also knew He was in control and was teaching me to trust Him more and more. Or maybe He was teaching me that I really did not trust Him. In the end, the outcome is the same. I trust, I do not trust, yet He continues to bid me to come and lay my burdens at His feet.

---

[4] Sandra Glahn and William Cutrer, M.D., *When Empty Arms Become a Heavy Burden* (Broadman & Holman Publishers, 1997), 208.

CHAPTER 4

Not too long after Elijah's birth, Micah left vocational ministry. We joined a new church where we could sit, be fed, and begin to understand the new way God was going to provide for our family. I was not prepared for this job path. Micah was given the opportunity to take his Bible degree and become a businessman. As it turns out, he was really good at it. It was an interesting time in life. It was a path we had to work out and pray about so much in the beginning as decisions were made that would affect our family for many years to come. Do not get me wrong, we were not called out of the ministry, just called out of ministry in a way that did not provide for our financial needs. Our new church was an answer to prayer. Very quickly, there were ways Micah was able to serve. We had a connectedness there that was such a gift.

One of the things we loved about our new church family was their focus on adoption. There was one couple in particular Micah and I grew to respect. They felt called to keep the church informed about opportunities to love orphans through a ministry called Just One. They were an adoptive family themselves and led by example. Micah and I attended an informational luncheon after worship one Sunday that highlighted different avenues for adoption. There were families that had adopted internationally, domestically, and also through something called embryo adoption. If you have never heard of this before, I am determined to tell you everything I know by the end of this book. At this time, I knew what embryo adoption was, it just did not seem to be our first choice.

I was introduced to embryo adoption the first time I ever stepped into the office of my reproductive endocrinologist. The seed had been planted early. I distinctly remember sitting with my doctor, discussing my second surgery and my prognosis. Lying on a table next to Micah was a pamphlet titled "Snowflake Adoption."[5] I was curious at first. While it was initially intriguing, the process of adopting embryos seemed intimidating. That is a nice word: intimidating. Terrifying is more the word I am thinking. I tried to suppress the thought of it. It burrowed into a place in my brain that was not easily choked out, and the concept sat there quietly for many years.

As much as we wanted to begin moving toward adoption, God was doing something different in our family and it was not the right time. With the Micah's new career trajectory, focus was necessary as our path was changing and becoming clearer and clearer.

In 2009, we began traveling as Micah had been accepted for a position to work in different places for relatively short periods of time all over the United States. Every place was new for our family. We drew closer to each other as geographical and relational familiarity was illusive. It was a great time to see how my big boys could adapt to new challenges and surroundings. Everything was an adventure. Andrew learned to read, Elijah too. I learned more about reading them and watching God continue to make them into unique individuals.

Even on the road, he and I continued to pray and talk about adoption as we, especially I, grieved knowing I would most likely never have another genetic child. The pain was real. Through the grief, the Lord kept moving

---

5 The Snowflakes® Embryo Adoption Program was established in 1997 by Nightlight® Christian Adoptions as the first embryo adoption program in the world.

in our hearts on behalf of orphans. We saw many friends adopt from other countries and from the U.S. It was such a joy to see children brought out of poverty, abuse, and neglect and birthed into homes full of love, loudly proclaiming their love for the One Who adopts us first. It all seemed beautiful. Our theology was also expanding to enlarge our thoughts about our own adoptions into the family of the God of the Bible. Everything about adoption sparked our own growing realizations of love and purpose. We read books about it. We resonated with it. We knew it was the next step. Micah and I talked and prayed for many months about which way to turn.

We began by praying through choosing a country from which to adopt; for example, Guatemala. It was strange. Almost immediately upon moving in that direction, adoptions were closed. After this happened twice, I began to research domestic adoptions. As an aside, I have always believed that God does not just give a family any child. He gives particular children to particular parents. It is not just some random selection of genes or personalities. It was my prayer that our child or children be revealed to us. I had confidence that God would guide us.

I knew the process for adopting and that a home study is inevitable for most situations. Our family moved six times that year. I remember thinking, "How are we ever going to be able to complete a home study when we cannot stay in one place longer than two months?" I knew traveling would come to an end, and I desired to be ready when the time was right, but that was impractical given the nature of home studies. There seemed to be doors closing all around us. Then, an option arose out of the blue.

My mom called me communicating an encounter she had with an acquaintance. This particular gal had a friend who wanted to give the child she was then expecting to another family through a private adoption. My mom's friend had been asked to help place that child in a loving home. She had relayed our information and story and felt the conversation should continue. I was put in touch with her acquaintance and did have contact for a substantial period of time. I did quite a lot of learning about adoption in general, and specifically private adoptions. It seemed to fit, given our circumstances. I prayed and asked God if He would have us love this child. More than expanding my understanding of legalities or systems, I learned about the life of this mother.

So often we see this glorious thing where orphans are given new homes, but there was something God impressed upon me during this time I had not considered before. Adoption is not only a beautiful bonding together of unlike people from different families. It first and always results from brokenness. I am not sure I had understood this as clearly before. This mother was a true representation of one who saw no other choice but to give her child to another mother. As a mother, I cannot imagine being in that position, feeling desperate to care for a child yet unable to do so. Micah and I, upon hearing her story, felt agonizingly sympathetic to her and she became a hero to us. There is something honoring about giving up someone you love who is inherently dear to you for the sake of his or her greater good. She, at the time, did not feel she could care for her child. Therefore, she had to separate herself from her baby. There is not a clearer picture of utter pain than a mother bodily separating from her child in whatever capacity. Before a family is built through adoption, there is separation. This is where adoption begins.

After months of discussion and even plans to give the mother housing and care during the time of the birth, she chose to keep the baby. We rejoiced and affirmed that we decidedly wanted to care for an orphan and not a child with an able parent or parents. At the same time, we wept. One cannot help but dream of what God is doing in these situations. I have learned to guard my heart against disappointment through years of sadness, yet to do so completely and without any expectation is humanly impossible. The more time passes, the more plans are made. Again, we wondered where God was going with all of this for us.

In 2010, Micah and I ended up making a full circle around the country. We moved six times in one year and we were so happy to end up back where we started, in Louisville, KY. With traveling behind us, Micah and I began to pursue adoption through a home for displaced children with which we had connections. In fact, when I was a young girl, my grandfather had included me in fundraisers for this particular ministry located right in my hometown. It seemed logical that this would be a place for us to be united to a child (or children) waiting on a forever family. Even with connections, the door closed there as well. It seemed the obvious choices for us were not options. It was all very confusing and our path was not plain for a long time. Still unsure of our final stop with Micah's job, all in the adoption arena seemed to halt.

I had filed away this other option — embryo adoption. From this point on, my views of life and personhood will be made as abundantly clear as I am able to make them. I am not going to leave you wondering.

In vitro fertilization has been around for decades. This is where embryo adoption begins.

In this method, embryos are the result of the joining of egg and sperm in a lab under controlled conditions. The egg is fertilized and within twelve hours, the nuclei merge, twenty-three maternal and twenty-three paternal chromosomes align and attach, and the child's DNA is then complete. It is at this point that I am absolutely convinced that a new person, made in the image of God, comes into being. The DNA is different than the DNA found in the cells of either parent, creating an entirely unique being. Those instructions are included in every cell as cells are divided, over and over again. In most in vitro fertilization cycles, embryos are matured to three or five days. Three-day-old embryos have four to eight cells. Five-day-old embryos are called blastocysts, distinguished by cellular differentiation[6]. It is up to the embryologist, or the scientist that oversees the joining of egg and sperm, what is ideal, especially considering if a couple is undergoing a fresh transfer (or in the same cycle in which the eggs are retrieved and fertilized) or if he or she will cryo-preserve embryos to be transferred in a later cycle. There are varying opinions as to what is best for the survival of the child (clinical term: achieve pregnancy). I certainly have my opinions, but I do not want to gloss over the real pain that leads a couple to choose IVF. It can be difficult wading in the waters of what we can do, humanly speaking, and what we should do. That is another topic to tackle in another book, another day.

Regardless of all the reasons, there are currently more than 600,000 cryo-preserved embryos in the U.S. alone. Why so many? Because harvesting and fertilizing eggs is expensive, many times there are more created than are allowed an opportunity to continue to grow. Not all frozen embryos are orphans. Many are still stored by their genetic parents. Most stored embryos (babies) will be given for research or left to thaw, unattended. Both of these result in the destruction of life. What to do when a couple reaches the end of the journey to a child or children and life still exists, called by their name in a storage lab, leaves them with difficult decisions. I have even read stories of couples that request to be buried with their remaining stored embryos.

When a couple (or individuals in some cases) goes through the process of IVF and has remaining embryos they will not be able to give a chance to continue to grow by transferring into a readied womb, they may choose to allow someone else that opportunity. They may relinquish their rights

---

[6] Alexander Tsiaras and Barry Werth, *From Conception to Birth* (Doubleday, 2002), 50-53.

to another family who then adopts the embryos. Clinically, this is referred to as embryo donation.

The reasons I think the term "embryo donation" is damaging and disparaging are better stated by Russell Moore. He has been writing about this for much longer than I.

> *Someone can donate sperm or ovum or even a heart or a liver, but no one can "donate" an "embryo." No one can "own" an "embryo." An "embryo" isn't a thing; he or she is a "who." Our Lord Jesus is the pinnacle of the image of God (Heb. 1:1-3). He was an "embryo" (Luke 1:42-43). The "embryonic" John responded to our Lord's "embryonic" presence in precisely the same way he responded to his adult presence on the banks of the Jordan River.*
>
> *These so-called "snowflakes" are brothers and sisters of the Lord Jesus are stored in cryogenic containers in fertility clinics as the "extras" of IVF projects. They already exist, and they already exist as persons created in the image of God.[7]*

I use the term "embryo adoption" because I desire to give honor, dignity, and respect to the process of bringing a child into a family other than his or her genetic family, just as I would any other kind of adoption. The word "adoption" calls an embryo a human being. It is not a legal term, however. Government regulations end in adoption when they would so clearly establish personhood.

---

[7] Moore, Russell, "Should Christians Adopt Embryos?" http://www.russellmoore.com/2012/09/20/should-christians-adopt-embryos/ (September 20, 2012).

Beyond the technical terminology and fascinating, mysterious way persons are conceived, I take Psalm 139 and other biblical texts literally. This one is especially compelling:

> *I praise you, for I am fearfully and wonderfully made.*
> *Wonderful are Your works; my soul knows it very well. My*
> *frame was not hidden from you when I was being made*
> *in secret, intricately woven in the depths of the earth. Your*
> *eyes saw my unformed substance; in Your book were written,*
> *every one of them, the days that were formed for me, when*
> *yet there was none of them.*[8]

Conception is our confirmation of a soul known by God. His thoughts always precede our knowledge. In all my limited understanding of theology and even embryology, I am convinced that persons are not accidents. I realized very early in reading and praying through discerning God's will for human life that "arbitrary" is not a proper description of His participation.

---

[8] Psalm 139:14-16

CHAPTER 5

The Lord kept calling to mind the option of embryo adoption. With all other doors closed, the nagging thought of adopting frozen ones sat like a rock in the pit of my stomach. I carried it around with me everywhere and saw it in every place. If you have had a calling to something you do not even understand completely, you may identify. It drew to mind all the things I feared the most as a mother—- pregnancy, conception, and the possibility of death. Really, I just wanted to run.

I recall a conversation I had with a friend even before traveling with my husband for his job. I had briefly mentioned embryo adoption over lunch and her reaction was a bit startling. I knew she and I shared the same beliefs regarding when life begins. I do not remember her exact words, but she implied that adopting embryos seemed less important than adopting children already living out in the world. I carried that conversation with me for a time and did a lot of soul searching on the issue. I believe there is some credence to the argument that those with consciousness and felt needs have a different level of emotional appeal than those who do not have those same immediate needs. Even so, after wrestling for a while, I began to feel especially convicted on the behalf of embryos. Sure, I was tempted to give myself an out, but her words had the opposite effect on me. Instead of being discouraged, I was more driven.

If I believe what I say I believe, then these embryos bear the image of their Creator. Each has a soul and days numbered before him or her, however many or few. As Micah and I thought and prayed, it seemed pressing that image bearers not remain in an indefinite state of suspended reality. The number of days they may or may not continue to grow was not my concern. At the very least, they must have a chance to live. To give them such an opportunity shows them honor and treats them as human beings. It began to seem cruel and inhumane to freeze persons indefinitely for the sake of reproductive rights. With questions come answers and then opinions. I began to see embryos who were not going to be given a chance at life like orphans without voices.

If we love Jesus, we are called to love those He loves. The Apostle James wrote that loving orphans and widows is true religion. After trying every other avenue we knew, Micah and I decided to begin pursuing these particular orphans. Given our story, it became the kind of admonition he and I were to either act upon or disobey. There was a particular morning sitting in worship that I knew the way I was to take. I do not even think what was happening in the service around me had anything to do with adoption; it was simply clear that I needed to take another step forward.

This warranted another email to Dr. C., my friend who always answered my sometimes-emotional emails within a day. He was in absolute agreement that I would be a good candidate for embryo adoption. With his affirmation, I had no other reason not to move forward. Amid the surrender was relief. I was thankful Micah was in agreement.

As I said before, the most difficult part of this obedience was the sobering reality that not all adopted embryos survive. If Micah and I love these little ones and desire to care for them as best we can, we may do so and never see their faces. Many cryo-preserved embryos do not even survive the thawing process. Others may survive but not implant and grow.

The process of preparing one's body to accept embryos beyond the natural order of reproduction involves much pain. That was not something I looked forward to, but losing little ones after praying for them to survive and becoming acquainted with their souls was almost more than I could bear to imagine. Experiencing infertility and miscarriage had taught me more than I wanted to know about the preciousness and painfulness of life. It was an area of my heart God had forced me to look into; that mixed, innate, God-glorifying desire – to mother – with pain and uncertainty. As much as I was afraid, God moved me.

One afternoon in the fall of 2010, I began researching the how-to's of embryo adoption. I remember sitting on the floor of my bedroom with the laptop, trying to navigate all the steps and options. I knew of two agencies that facilitated these adoptions. As I read and reread all I could find over the internet, it all seemed more daunting. The cost alone was staggering. Then, there were multiple stages and steps, applications and more applications. My head was spinning, and it all felt too overwhelming. As I tried to steady my gaze on the goal instead of the details I prayed, "God, if this is what you have for us, You are going to have to make it easier than this."

In all my reading, it was made clear that if we went with one particular agency, I would have to be diagnosed as infertile as their philosophy mainly served those couples. Since I do have secondary infertility, I emailed the agency asking if my diagnosis would suffice. I would need a clear label that signified my inability to conceive in order to adopt embryos. I called my doctor; the same reproductive endocrinologist who had performed two surgeries for me and first introduced me to "Snowflake Adoption." I needed him to do me the honor of providing written verification of my heart-piercing, embryo-adoption-required diagnosis. His receptionist returned my call later the same day and while on the phone, I happened to mention seeing the embryo adoption pamphlet years ago. I did not even know how his particular office could help or would be involved in these adoptions. I wondered if they simply referred interested couples to an agency. Her reply was a direct answer to my specific prayer.

"I don't know how many embryos we have available now, Mrs. Childs," said the receptionist on the other end of the line, "but you can come in for a consult in a couple of weeks if you'd like." I was dumbfounded. As I sit here writing this, I hear her words echoing in my head and I doubt they will ever disappear. I began asking questions. By this time, I had an arsenal. No home study... no applications... we just come in and choose our embryos. Because of the lack of governmental oversight due to the fact that embryos are not recognized as persons, the process through the clinic was rather simple. I was ecstatic to take full advantage of the simplicity.

I got off the phone and immediately called Micah. We had an appointment in two weeks. Calm and collected, he said, "Okay."

I do not know how God works in the secret, mysterious things. I do know from scripture there is a cosmic drama that entertains the angels as they watch my story of redemption from their seats in the world unseen. I grew up in a Southern Baptist church where people did not speak in tongues or receive words of prophecy, and I am not sure how you, dear reader, will hear what I am about to say: Heaven kissed my life with an undeniable, perceivable hope that day. My heart was encouraged in a most unique way. I know now, looking back, I would draw from this kind of encouragement in the months following. God knew, ordained, and followed through in causing His name to be known in my soul in a way that I could not deny from that day forward.

We Grow (by God's Grace) and Our Family Grows (The letter we sent to our families and friends):

As many of you know, we have felt called to adopt since the beginning of our marriage. Adoption is one of the most beautiful pictures given to us by God to illustrate our relationship with Him in Christ our Redeemer, once separated from God but now called sons of the Father (Galatians 4:1-6). Little did we know that God had a very specific, personal road to walk down in pursuit obeying this calling and desire.

We have struggled with how much of this road we will share with you, but we feel peacefully led to a place of more full disclosure. It is clear to us that God has put us on this path and we want to testify to His work in our lives, so bear with us as we share a little of our journey. We have been given two precious miracles in our boys, Andrew and Elijah. The road for us to have biological children was paved with much waiting, miscarriage, and some medical intervention. While we know that God can do anything and believe that we don't always know what is around the corner, the door has seemed to close for us to have more biological children despite the same treatments since the birth of Elijah. Honestly, we have wrestled with this, but knew God was writing... He has the pen. He knows our hearts and has heard every prayer. He has provided more for us than we deserve, and does all things for His glory and for our good out of love for us. We always were clear in our personal convictions regarding fertility treatments. They are very expensive and we always agreed that if we felt that God might expand our family more, instead of putting money toward more treatments we would use the money for adoption.

In the past few months, adoption has moved up on our priority list. We have had peace in waiting patiently this past year as we moved all over the country with Chick-fil-A but are now in a position where we can focus our attention on praying for what our part would be in caring for orphans. There are many different ways to adopt and so many orphans, it can be overwhelming discerning which direction to go. We first felt led to adopt from Ebenezer's Children's Home in Wilkesboro, NC. This seemed to be feasible until we found out we would be back in Louisville, 8 hours away. When that option seemed to be out of the question, we prayed about where to turn next.

Several years ago, we had been introduced to embryo adoption by a pamphlet in a doctor's office and then later through an adoption informational luncheon at our church. When we first heard about it, it seemed interesting but probably not for us. Honestly, my first thought was, "Why would couples adopt embryos when there are so many children that need families all over the world?" When I would bring up the question with friends, about half of the time, that was the same response. Why do this?

Slowly and gently, the Lord starting giving us clarity in how to think of these "snowflake" babies. As a result of the number of couples seeking to have biological children through in-vitro fertilization, there are currently more than 400,000 (possibly more than 500,000) cryo-preserved embryos in the US. Many of the couples who had these babies "created" in a lab have met their "family goals" and have no further use for the embryos. If we believe what we say we believe, that all humans are bearers of the image of God from conception, then these little cryo-preserved babies are little frozen orphans. They have no breath yet; no voice for themselves. Many (and we daresay most) of these embryos will never get a chance at life. After varying amounts of storage time, couples are given choices as to how they are to be "used" or disposed of. There are some couples who donate their embryos for stem cell extraction and research and others that allow their embryos — their babies — to be destroyed. However, there are couples who donate their embryos for other couples to "adopt." Of course our government does not see this as true adoption, because that would be calling an embryo a human.

Because of all our struggles with infertility, we are perfect candidates for embryo adoption. Couples who are not diagnosed as infertile (or in our case, with secondary infertility) are many times not even considered as candidates for embryo adoption. That makes the opportunity for those able to adopt embryos more scarce. There are Christian adoption agencies that handle matching embryo donors with adopting families, but in our case with Tiffany's medical history, we are adopting directly through the clinic and physician here in Louisville that helped her years ago. The doctor and office staff love facilitating embryo adoptions and the care we have been given so far has been tender and precious.

Please pray that those of us who value life will respond in a God-honoring way toward this group of precious babies, frozen in time, but known by their True Creator. He loves each and every one! Secondly, we really need your prayers. We want to be very clear about our expectations about this process. We are trusting that God has led us to this place, has gone before us, and is abounding in all the things we will need over the coming months. We will be experiencing some of the challenges that couples who choose IVF will face so there are definitely some physical and emotional needs. Also, pray for our four little embryos! Pray that God would prepare them as He is preparing us for this adoption. JIOJ
~ October 25, 2010

CHAPTER 6

※

I was handed a manila folder. It was open and I started flipping through the pages... this couple, that couple, this age, that race, this occupation, that blood type. I felt overwhelmed. How do I choose? Thankfully, Micah was right next to me. I handed him the folder. He picked a paper from the stack. "This is what I think," he said. "Four is a good number." It took me a minute to wrap my head around the choice, but I was so glad the choice was made. "They want diversity!" the Nurse Practitioner reported to the doctor. A "Transfer of Property" in the eyes of the law. Medication- check. Visit to the financial office- check. Next appointment made- check. The whole appointment took less than an hour. JIOJ ~ Oct. 27, 2010

The first time I entered the reproductive endocrinologist's office as a patient to adopt embryos, I was thankful for the familiarity. I described the experience as like being in a Christian science fiction movie. The atmosphere was like no other doctor's office: the dim lights, the soft-spoken words of the receptionist, the health-oriented magazines, etc. It was all familiar territory, but I was entering with a new history and my gear was remarkably different.

Many years before, Micah and I had considered if and when my endometriosis would inhibit childbearing, what we would do to intervene. The last two times I had entered this office, I was a patient being treated for a particular diagnosis. We were in agreement that endo is a physical disease that requires treatment for various reasons. My past surgeries were the best treatments given my specific symptoms and issues and, at those junctures, it had not progressed to disallow childbearing. Of all the physicians I could trust with my care, I gained a large degree of respect for this particular reproductive endocrinologist. He was (and is) knowledgeable, kind, and respectful of my personal convictions. He never pushed me to make a decision to do a more aggressive treatment that would make me uncomfortable. Beyond treating my cycle issues and endo, Micah and I were unanimous in our decision to put any and all time, energy, and money toward adoption should those treatments come to an end.

Most of all, this doctor was the first person to introduce me to embryo adoption. During my first appointment, I was ushered into the even more quiet room in the midst of the examination rooms of the clinic. The room itself had a living room feel with a sofa, armoire and TV, coffee table, side table, and all the dressings of relax. At my first visit with this doctor, I glanced through a pamphlet regarding Snowflake Adoption on the side table. I was intrigued enough to make a brief inquiry. My doc's response was simply one of affirmation of their participation, whatever that meant. Back then, I did not ask any more questions. I grabbed the pamphlet and tucked it inside my purse.

Now, I entered as a candidate for embryo adoption. I had made a good-sized circle in coming to this place. This visit, we skipped the living room where I had first been introduced and went straight to the conference room. The nurse practitioner discussed the formalities rather quickly. At this point in time, I had done so much research and I was well prepared with what it would take to go forward. Micah and I spoke with knowledge and understanding, which was helpful navigating the simply-stated, yet complex, conversation. With that, we were given our options of those embryos available to be adopted.

I was surprised at just how easy it was. I could not help but wonder about the families represented in that folder. I knew each of their roads had been laden with the heartache of infertility. I felt so thankful they chose to honor the lives of their little ones in allowing them to be adopted. I know just how easy it would be for them to have chosen differently. Other parts of me wished there were not so many left in limbo in the first place. Then I was reminded of all the ones in contrast who would live in a state of suspended reality indefinitely. It was so difficult for me to choose one family over another and I was so thankful my husband was up to that task.

Our first four adopted embryos were from a family of an entirely different race than both Micah and me — and we loved that. Honestly, I was thankful that God would choose to more fully express His love for all peoples within our family in that way. One sheet of paper described our children, all bundled together by their shared DNA.

With a multitude of emotions, I left that office the mother of seven. Suddenly, I was concerned about all the things mothers are concerned over for my little ones. I started thinking about where they were stored and how they would be kept safe until I could care for them. I was ready to love them and honor their lives in the best way I possibly could.

In this quick time, we grew to hold these babies, like we hold
our own boys, in our hearts. They won't have our DNA, but

will hopefully grow in my belly and be born into our family in the same way as Andrew and Elijah. What an amazing thought. Our days are spent praying for them. When we speak of them being frozen Andrew asks, "Do you think they are cold, Mommy?" Right now they don't feel the cold, but we can't wait until they feel the warmth of being given a chance to live. When people ask how many children we have now, Micah is the first to answer "6 — in this world." JIOJ ~ Oct. 27, 2010

CHAPTER 7

Micah and I went for our pre-transfer appointment to make sure I was physically ready to give a gestational home to our little ones. Within a short time, the nurse practitioner identified issues, specifically a type of ovarian cyst, that had to be treated before anything else could proceed. Surgery was scheduled before the end of that week and the regimen of hormones and medications would need to begin. In God's perfect timing, my mother-in-law was in town and available to help out. The procedure was successful and remarkably, relatively painless in every way for me. I recovered quickly and was motivated to press on with our plan.

In the weeks following surgery, I grew accustomed to the medications that would prepare my body to carry babies in the most natural, cyclical way. There was a series of hormones and other meds that took control of my cycle, so that the timing of the transfer would be optimal. I was nervous that first month, especially with the injections. I was completely comfortable giving injections to someone else, but not so sure about giving them to myself. The first ones were given in my abdomen and did not prove to make me feel bad at all. Then came the Intra-muscular Progesterone. Because of the location of the injection site, I was convinced that Micah needed to be the one to administer them. It was painful for me, but I think more painful for him (or upon further reflection, maybe not).

There is the idea of something, and then there is the execution of that something. The idea of having 1.5" needles stuck into an area behind my scope of vision by my non-medically-trained husband is one thing and quite another to have him do it every day, twice a day. Then there came the day when there were more knots than free space within the small target injection area and the swelling did not have a chance to subside, even though I was alternating sites. I began to lose feeling in parts of my hips, and the surrounding areas ached constantly. It hurt to lean back in a chair to relax or to lie down. It was brutal. Micah always treated this as, "I really don't want to do this to you but it is what is necessary... so I will be as gentle as possible... but you may need to suck it up for right now and let me get it over with, dear." It was a real marriage builder.

With another trip for a sonogram, we were both pleased by the fruit of our labor. All of those hormones, in cooperation with my anatomy, did create a favorable environment for growing babies. That final pre-transfer trip to the doctor's office and ultrasound confirmed that we were ready.

Something quite remarkable happened in my big boys in this whole process. Micah and I both felt strongly that we would be open about as much as we could with the two of them. We started with a lesson about reproduction in general, simplified terms and then went on to try and explain the medical assistance side of the whole thing. They were either really, really confused or open-heartedly accepting of it all. Andrew in particular desired a bigger family, and so he was thrilled that he would be a big brother to more Childs children. They grew to be such a dear support. On days when I was unable to articulate my heart for the children in our care, Andrew and Elijah would do it with conviction and childlike faith over their PB&J. They prayed for their siblings. They asked about them. They were very patient with me. They both became the most tender big brothers. I was in awe of the way they honored the lives of our little ones along with us.

After the weeks of preparation, the day arrived for us to go to the clinic to have the embryos, thawed just that morning, transferred into my womb. We arrived, prayerful and curious about what all this would entail. The clinic was doing several transfers that morning and there were curtains separating Micah and me from the other couples there for the same procedure. After donning hospital attire, we met our nurse, nurse practitioner, and the embryologist who had cared for our little ones that morning. As the embryologist approached my bed, I saw in her hand two individual pictures of our children. She laid them on my lap with a cheery, "Here they are!" It was so strange, yet fascinating to see them so early in their development. They were five days old when they had been cryo-preserved. After a brief wait time, I was wheeled into a small room with an adjoining window to another room where our embryos were waiting.

After proper positioning of both Micah and me, I glanced above me where I was greeted by a cover on the overhead light with clouds and flowers. I do not know if it was meant to bring peace or amusement in my awkward state! At least my husband was at my side. Our doctor retrieved the embryos, and in just a few seconds, they were transferred. After a confirmation by the embryologist that the embryos had exited their occupied space and were now in my belly, I was wheeled back into the main room with the other couples.

There, still and quiet, I "held" my babies. They were out of the cold lab, were with me, and they were growing.

The quiet was broken as another couple was wheeled to the area next to us. As soon as they were settled in for their post-transfer wait, they began asking questions of the nurse and nurse practitioner. Their questions were surprising and curious to me.

We overheard, as you just cannot help but overhear when there is nothing but a dividing curtain between you, a conversation during those thirty minutes that has altered my understanding of what might go on in the minds of those pursuing IVF. Minutes from their first transfer, the couple kindly asked what would happen to their remaining embryos if this cycle was a success and they were able to deliver a baby. The NP explained their options, highlighting embryo adoption. I guess the first thing that surprised me was that this would be the first time they would ask this question. It was very discouraging to hear that this had not been a concern until just this moment.

Upon hearing this, I learned two things: 1) Not everyone goes into IVF with an understanding of all it entails. 2) Not everyone has a plan for all embryos created. Perhaps they did not even know they had a choice as to how many were "created" in the first place. I knew for a fact, this particular clinic was conservative in the number of eggs they allowed to be fertilized; however, there were still too many for couples to care for in some cases, clearly.

After our wait time, my nurse came over to give us instructions regarding the days following. She had a gentle way about her that was so calming. She asked if we needed anything. All I could say was that I wished for her to pray for our babies. With a smile, she gladly agreed.

I went home and felt as though I was most fragile. Micah supplied my favorite meal and gave me the opportunity to relax. There were a few days of bed rest. I had a sweet friend who came over and spent that portion with me. She made me dinner and brought movies. I needed distraction, nutrition, and rest, and God provided it all through her in a sweet way.

The wait was outwardly peaceful but inwardly maddening. Am I still pregnant? Is that a symptom?

I recalled the scripture to think on things that are true and focus on the fact that the last I knew, our babies were growing and thriving. I would speak to them, those things I whisper to my children in the dark. I sang to them in the quiet of the evening or in the car as I carried them along. Whatever my time with them, I would do my best to introduce myself and let them know how very much they were loved. I knew they could not hear me, but it did not matter. I cared for the vessel that held them. I knew all the recommendations for pregnant women, and I did not want to compromise anything that might make me feel guilt later. I wanted so badly to care for them as long as God would allow.

My husband and big boys continued to pray for them, for each one. It was important to me that we were not only praying for a continued pregnancy, but for each child to continue to live and grow. They joined me in this plea. They treated me with tenderness and care.

The day before I was to go in for my post-transfer appointment, I took a pregnancy test at home. There was a risk in testing early. I could get a false result not waiting the desired amount of time, but I remember wanting some heads-up before being subject to public knowledge. With my heart racing, I took the test. The result was negative.

The next day (three days before Christmas), Micah and I went into the office for our official test, at twelve days post-transfer. I do not remember much of the drive there, I just remember being back on that sofa in the extra quiet room. I remember shaking heads and choking back tears until I had a bit of privacy.

Even before we left the office, I was already thinking toward our other embryos still waiting. I was simultaneously wading into the waters of deep grief as I said goodbye to our precious two who had spent some time with us.

There is an attachment that occurs from the first moment the faint line appears on the pregnancy test. For me, I did not need a test. I knew there had been five-day-old babies suspended in time in a lab and for me as the one caring for them, the possibilities for the ways they would inhabit my family were endless. Those thoughts for them had shifted to the present reality of them peacefully entering eternity.

As I walked in the door of our apartment, I fell into the arms of my friend Becky. God provided in her a most dear soul who grieved with us and simply allowed me to cry on her shoulder. I shared the news with Andrew and Elijah. They were sad. I wanted to help them through their sadness. Soon after telling them their siblings were gone, Elijah so sweetly reminded his mommy, "Being here with us is good, but being with God is better." Sometimes, my children lead me.

Our little ones are no longer with us, but are safe in the arms of the Father. I can only imagine their little faces — eyes opening for the first time to see the face of Jesus — being surrounded by everlasting, perfect love. We grieve, but not as those who have no hope. We look forward to knowing them throughout eternity. We sure are going to miss them until then. It has been such a privilege carrying them, even for such a short time. JIOJ ~ December 22, 2010

CHAPTER 8

This past week, we learned that our last two embryos from the group of four we originally adopted aren't in the best condition. There are systems by which embryologists grade embryos. The systems are subjective and vary from clinic to clinic but serve the purpose of deciding which embryos are "competent." Sometimes, incompetent embryos are discarded. Since we firmly believe that all embryos, regardless of their grade, should be given a chance at life, we are glad to know our clinic has reserved that dignity for them. It does cause us to pray for them even more and seek the Lord for His supernatural help for them. There is more to this story, however.

It all started at my last doctor visit. Micah and I spoke with the nurse about adopting a third embryo to transfer. This was even before the news of the condition of our other two. It would be a lone embryo, we assumed, as there were several families with only one left and donated. We went back and forth for a while, listing the pros and cons. It is so strange, this whole process — weighing statistics, facts, and assumptions versus walking with the God who holds all things together by the word of His power — The God who we call Father who moves in a mysterious way, His wonders to perform. The God who makes the blind see, the lame walk, the deaf hear, and the dead live again. We left the appointment with the intention to pray about it and let them know our decision sometime before the transfer. Since then, we have prayed a lot and sought wisdom from other friends and family. Really, the question I kept asking myself was, "Can I pray for all of these babies — each one — that they all will live and mean it?" The question is legitimate. It would not be easy for us to care for triplets or, more importantly, good for them sharing a limited growing space. The chance of them all surviving is very slim from a historical/ statistical standpoint. Again, human understanding — All-Powerful Lord. We did decide it would be a wise use of the transfer cycle for us to go ahead with three, praying for each of them to live. I decided to let the office know our intentions the day of our final appointment before the transfer.

Enter our friends Josh and Danae. Josh and Danae are the sister and brother-in-law of my friend, Cara. Shortly after we began our embryo adoption, they were led to pursue the same thing. Danae and I are both scheduled for our embryo transfers within a couple of days of each other; this being our second cycle and their first. They had adopted a group of seven embryos. They had chosen them because they were deemed the "least adoptable" of all the embryos donated at our clinic. Danae sent me a text message last week asking if I'd talked with our clinic about adding another embryo.

At this point, I had not. Danae said she got a call from the nurse practitioner asking to "use" one of their embryos for a transfer scheduled for another adopting couple who fit our profile. Danae was glad to have another family willing to help give all of hers a chance at life, since seven is a large number to take on, given a more conservative approach. It was a concern to her and Josh that there would come a point in time where they might have to decide to relinquish one or more to be adopted. In talking to Danae, it was already like talking to a mom trying to decide the best for her children, even with all the unknowns in front of her. Danae even offered, if the other couple wasn't us, to allow us to transfer another of theirs. She and Josh certainly have those little ones in mind — wanting each one to be cared for.

Even after our conversation, I was not convinced the couple the NP was speaking of was us. When Danae called in tears, I was proved completely wrong! The clinic had gotten the news of the condition of our embryos and was working on our behalf to add a third. Unknown to our mutual NP, the solution she provided made Josh and Danae and Micah and me the parents of these siblings. She had no idea we knew each other. JIOJ ~ Feb. 6, 2011

Micah and I had a scheduled trip to San Antonio and with a bag full of syringes (my new traveling companions), we went cautiously through airport security. Toward the end of the trip, I began the medications needed to best care for the little ones who would later be transferred. It is funny now to think of all the places I have given myself shots—- in closets, on airplanes, crazy-germy public restrooms. Ick! There was so much out of my control, the least I could do was make sure I got all of my meds on time. I also enjoyed sharing with others the road ahead of us. It is not the most natural thing to bring up in conversation, but it has always felt disingenuous to not fully answer a continual line of questioning about the members of my family. It is funny, you can almost immediately tell how a conversation is going to go in just a few seconds. Some people hear "embryo adoption" and they say, "Ohhh..." and that is it. Others are curious. If you show any signs of curiosity, you may get more than you bargained for, because I will tell you things. Probably more than you wanted to know.

Just a few days after arriving back home and in February 2011, Micah and I arrived at the clinic for a second time to see who survived the thawing process and give them a happy home. Upon our arrival at the clinic for this, our second transfer, we learned that one from the group from whom our friends Josh and Danae had adopted and another from our original four did not survive. Those two were no longer suspended in time, but with Jesus. Another from our shared group and the last one from our first group of four did survive. These would be the two I would carry as long as the Lord would allow. I looked at their photographs and imagined delivering two babies, from two different races, and the thought made me smile. In just a few minutes, they were both tucked away and prayed over. There is a sigh of relief that washes over a mommy when her babies have all been cared for. I was so grateful they were free to be whatever God would have them be, no longer in suspension.

Then the waiting began again. My time with these babies was sweet and quiet. Again I was on bed rest for a few days, followed by more waiting. I shared some hopeful conversations with Danae. Her transfer had gone well and she too was anticipating the end of our twelve-day wait. I knew inevitably some answers would be coming and I wanted to handle them appropriately. In some ways, I did not want those days to end or have to deal with death, again. I just did not want to know. Ignorance is sometimes bliss.

The pain of our losses was still fresh and I dreaded having to go through it again. I prayed and prayed. I sang and rocked. I packed as much into those days as a mommy can. With reluctance and hopefulness, I again took a home test to prepare what would probably preface our post-transfer visit to the RE office. The test was, again, negative. The visit confirmed that our little ones had gone to be with Jesus. Returning from the doctor's office, Micah and I pulled into the parking space outside our apartment. As I wept, the clouds wept with us. The gray from the sky enveloped the geography around me, creating tones illustrating the depth of our sadness. Creation was weeping with me.

Again, Becky was there to share in our mourning.

Fairly soon, I was anxious to check in with Danae. I will never forget sitting down in the rocking chair and hearing her voice on the other end of the line. Very quickly into the conversation, I sensed that the substance of our words would not be light. She had taken a pregnancy test and it was positive. Out of the same family of embryos, at least one of Danae's had continued to grow — ours had not. The news came as a surprise. Her first post-transfer appointment was not for a couple of days, but she had tested early. From what I remember, I spent the conversation reassuring her I was okay and rejoicing at the continued life given one or both of her little ones. While trying to remain lucid through overwhelming emotion, my head was spinning. I had become well acquainted with feeling sad for me yet happy for someone else simultaneously, but this new degree of compartmentalization cut me to the core. I knew this situation was extremely trying for Danae as well. I am not completely sure of all I said to her, but I know in hindsight I was limp in the arms of my Shepherd as we spoke.

My response to everything here has changed my understanding of my life and the work of my Father forever.

I got off the phone, and the pain sank in. I sank with it. There was no more energy for defense or protection from the pain I was feeling. There were no Bible verses or songs to serve as analgesics. There was no quiet space in my soul. I had been stripped of any protective garment and was bare before the Most Holy One. The pain was unbearable.

I turned into a thunder and lightning storm of words, thoughts, and emotions. I remember very clearly standing in my shower pounding on the wall until my palm turned red and swollen. It was a time when my limits of suffering were tested; when I felt I might die of a broken heart. What astonishes me the most in thinking back about this type of suffering was the culmination of both circumstantial suffering and suffering my soul felt as I encountered a new depth of my brokenness.

Yes, I was sad for the loss of these children. I was sad there are so many frozen babies locked away in sterile containment rooms all over the world. I was angry so many mothers choose to end the lives of their babies. I had righteous anger. I was mourning the loss of children, again. I had carried and buried these babies to the very best of my ability. There were other things — more frightening things — coming out of me. I no longer held inside thoughts and feelings directed toward God for fear of seeming unfaithful. It all came spilling out. I was angry God had called me to this suffering. I was angry I had been called to carry these precious ones to their death by my Father who knew the depth of the pain I had already experienced. He had cared for them through me, but what about me? As much as I wanted to rejoice, I was upset that Danae was pregnant and I was not. That kind of hypocrisy was soul shattering. I wanted so badly to feel my babies in my arms and see their faces. I wanted a happy announcement; not another loss. I did not want to go the rest of my life with no visible representation of our adoptions. Others might not know of this (good) thing I had done, and I would have to keep this all inside. Despair was imminent, and pride a poor comforter.

Then there was the way I should be behaving. I wish I could say that I, with faithful resolve, accepted this lot and portion from the Lord. I wish I had been found praising God in these circumstances! I should be thanking Him for the suffering. I should be grateful that He had added to our family as I had asked. I should... I should... I should... but I did not. I knew all the right, God-honoring things to think and say and be that would help me hold the course of belief. Years of learning God's word informed what I knew to be God-honoring. Yet, how could I do it all?

There are days when I have energy to hide, but on this day, I knew. This is a part of who I am. I knew for sure God would turn His back on me in disappointment. I was suddenly just like those in scripture most rebuked. I felt like I had been obedient and I deserved something good for it. Reciprocation was what I thought I desired. I wanted to hold my faith and obedience up to God and see it repaid with living children. I did not want to do the right thing anymore and just wanted to hold my babies... I knew it, God knew it, and I knew that He knew it. I was not sure how He was going to respond to my anger and pride directed toward Him.

If God had disclosed our entire job description when He first called Micah and me to adopt embryos — highlighting the sacrifices required to show love, dignity, and respect to our six little ones in order to bring them directly to Him in the end — I know deep in my heart I may not have been so quick to obey. In fact, I think I may have tried to run away... far,

far away in the opposite direction. That has never worked out for anyone I know throughout history, so I must assume that it would have not worked out so well for me. Honestly, for the first time in days, I can say in retrospect that I would without a doubt do it all over again. Even though God has added to our family in a way we never expected, He has honored our request for more children. It gives the phrase "treasures in heaven" a far deeper meaning to all of us. JIOJ
~ March 20, 2011

As for Danae, she and I share a unique bond I will always treasure. Just a few weeks later, she found out that she had been carrying one little one of her two transferred. Sadly, a few weeks later, that child also went on to be with Jesus.

CHAPTER 9

As a child and adolescent, I was taken every week to church. My pastor was my grandfather and I heard Bible teaching from someone I knew loved me. He was very passionate about the scriptures and he faithfully shared the gospel every week. I heard that Jesus died to save sinners over and over again. I cannot remember a time that I was not sensitive to the message of the gospel.

When I was seven years old, I knew God had saved me. I knew that I did not do what He said for me to do in His Word. I was a liar, unloving (especially toward my younger sister, whom I tormented with both sisterly affection and disdain), disobedient to my parents, and characteristically stubborn. In life in general, I wanted my own way and was savvy in getting it. This was the extent to which God's law met me, an adolescent. I had learned Bible lessons about how to and, more often, not to behave like most of the characters found in its pages. I felt conviction for how I did not make the right choices. I felt great about my good choices. They did not carry consequences and usually came along with praise. There were also lessons about Jesus and how to follow Him. I was happy that I could go to be with God in heaven and not be punished eternally in hell.

What I knew of Christianity as a teenager and young adult centered around the admonishment that because I knew Jesus, I should be a good person. I was not too concerned with my not-so-easily exposable sins and usually ignored them. I wanted my faith and life to be seen as light to others. I was not quick to admit whatever might make me seem unchristian. When something was exposed about me that might suggest some sin, I was very quick to defend, deflect, or hide it. I was also moved to desire to do good things. It made my parents and teachers proud of me and I grew to constantly look for affirmations that I was okay. I always felt affirmed when others deemed me a good Christian girl. I went on youth retreats and silently rededicated my life to Jesus over and over again. I threw out all my secular music. I served as president of the Fellowship of Christian Athletes. I signed a True Love Waits card. My spiritual life was defined by the decisions I was making and became my post-salvation experience identity. It worked until my choices were deemed inarguably not-so-good.

Married at age eighteen, my identity shifted to striving to become the Proverbs 31 woman and ever-submissive wife. I was fairly good at it in some ways and completely horrible in others. Again, me... what I was doing... there is a theme here.

When Micah and I were in seminary I had many years behind me of learning God's Word, but none so intense as our time within those walls. One thing for which I am so thankful was teaching that expounded upon the magnitude of God. I was most drawn to descriptions of the triune God that described Him in self-sustained, no-one-can–mess-it-up glory with the right to be worshiped and adored. I loved the thought that He was in control as adulthood changed what could be to what actually is and seemed so out of my control. The sovereignty of God gave me a peace outside of me and was easily identifiable as I began to reflect on my own history even in limited life experience. God had always pursued me and my life was a testimony. My response toward God was always a desire to do what God said for me to do.

If an entire culture and community inundated with persons called to ministry did anything, it persuaded me in the direction of more of the right things to do. As exposure to the full counsel of God's Word grew, my knowledge of the Bible and the importance of Christian obedience grew. I also learned the right heart attitudes to have. Sermon after sermon, Bible lesson after Bible lesson, I learned how to distill scriptures into manageable portions so I could keep track of my successes and failures in outward and inward obedience. Sometimes I was fairly successful. From the outside, I did a lot of God-honoring things. The Christian life was mostly defined by Bible truths that, many times, worked themselves out in discernment, defining what I was for or against, how well I knew the Bible to back up my faith, the way to systematically witness, how to practice spiritual disciplines, etc. I could do a good portion of this stuff I thought, for the most part.

There were some teachings that always convicted me, though. Learning right heart attitudes always felt condemning. I was sure that pride was in me somewhere, maybe everywhere. I did not like the way Jesus spoke to the religiously prideful. I knew what I was thinking each time I felt biblically successful, and it was scary. I was always measuring my faith by my obedience and the result was either depressing (when I felt I was doing poorly) or conversely satisfying (when I felt as if I was doing well), and I would quickly forget God until I needed Him again.

Do not get me wrong, I did love and trust Jesus. My love for Him (or as I now understand, my knowledge of His love for me) was only ever proportionate to my understanding of just how far off the mark I was as I lived out life in service to Him. My identity as a believer in Jesus Christ orbited around my estimation of how well I was doing at what God has called me to do and be. It completely dominated my thoughts. I still did not know what to do when my desires did not materialize in perfect obedience in actions and attitudes.

This was the most palpable in my soul during the years Micah and I struggled through infertility. I had a very difficult time keeping my Christianity in check after having the Bible expounded to illuminate the discontented places of my heart, yet still call me to mother children. There were two thoughts I had regarding children and family that are biblical. First, it is honorable for a woman to desire to be a mother. From Genesis, God calls Adam and Eve to be fruitful and multiply. Secondly, idolatry is clearly condemned. The definition of idolatry is much broader than merely bowing to a wooden statue. In relation to motherhood, I should not make childbearing an idol or, to say it another way, to desire children more than I desire God. The descriptions of idolatry were clear and come down directly from the mountain. Good Christians avoid breaking those laws especially!

I did not always know how to measure the mandate for married couples to populate the earth, the creation of women with a propensity in their DNA to love and nurture children, descriptions of mothers and mothering in honoring ways, and condemnation for wanting all of that too much. I was confused sometimes by what might constitute idolatry in a culture where advances in reproductive technology are helpful, yet push the envelope to areas not addressed so clearly in scripture (or in consistent interpretations). The juxtaposition of scriptures about asking and receiving, faith, trust, full-quivers, and rejoicing in suffering causes a gal trying to reorient her thoughts, advised by the full counsel of God in scripture, to become quite paralyzed. Integrating all relevant teachings all the time seemed impossible, and I just wanted to do the right thing. I also knew that even though choices might be right, heart attitudes still condemn.

In the years after God had given me my sweet boys, marriage and parenthood provided a "rubber meets the road" that most consequentially expounded biblical thoughts about God's demands for women. I studied how to be a biblical wife and mother, as these identities were most congruent with my calling. I knew my attempts would be imperfect, but I would try nonetheless. I did always carry with me the feeling that God was more or less disappointed with me as I related to my closest neighbors — my husband and children. When things did not go like the books or some of my friends said they should, I felt like I was doing something wrong (I was). I was sure that if I had a clearer knowledge of what was required of me in this life, I could do a better job at doing it. This worked itself out in varying ways. Instead of making me better and more successful, I began to see just how much struggle is encapsulated in these precious relationships. If sermons gave lists of ways I could love my husband and love my children, I was pretty good at putting their suggestions into practice. I am usually functional that way.

Parenting seemed to be the most difficult. It was the second most important of my jobs, and the one I had most fought to gain. I learned biblical language and ways to communicate holistic Christian living to my little ones, exposing sin in actions and attitudes. As soon as words left my mouth in admonishments to my children, I always knew God was also speaking to me. All the things I repeated to them day after day highlighted where my problems really reside — within my heart — and I was continually accused. Even as I corrected my big boys in their early childhood years, I felt the most conviction I had ever felt in regards to my own lack of obedience in the areas I insisted they obey.

I love that God made me a wife and mother. These titles speak to me in ways others do not and never will. However, they are the things I succeed and fail in the most as they tempt me to forget God and my need for

Him. I once had a dear friend look me in the eyes and tell me I was a perfect mother in Christ Jesus. No one had ever spoken to me like this before. I may have heard — not explicitly, but implicitly — many times, "Because you are in Christ, be a perfect (or next to perfect) mother."

I did not even know what to do with such a thought. I knew it spoke to a parched and desperate part of my soul and was a different word than I was used to hearing. I will never forget the hope it brought, the life it breathed. Once I shared it with another gal who asked, "What does that mean?" At the time I was not completely sure, but I hoped it was true.

Looking back, what appears to have been happening in the life of a gal loved by God and informed by His Word was that the law of God was growing to be bigger than what was inscribed on stones. All this time, I was learning about God and who He is. In stark contrast, I was also learning about who I am. The Bible is full of law, our culture is full of law, and it was crushing me.

The law had been given, handed down from the mountain, nuanced throughout the prescriptions of the Bible, and written on my softened heart in sermon after sermon, Bible lesson after Bible lesson. It felt progressively heavy. Knowing more of it is not freeing or enabling; it is condemning. It does give ways to think about the sufferings of life and the way God designed it to function without consequences. I agreed there is sin, suffering, and circumstance, but defining each of them respectively did not make me any more confident in always dividing them correctly. It also did not make me sin less. There was always another law to learn, another plan to apply.

The process of adopting and then losing babies was where the Law of God ushered me to my first, more biblically informed end. There had been instilled in me a deep-rooted desire, and even a calling I was sure was God given, to adopt. If there is anything a Christian should be about, it is caring for orphans and widows. God had given me years of writing His Word on my heart including the exhortation from James 1:27 describing how pure and undefiled religion operates. Loving others, particularly orphans and widows, fulfills the law and the prophets in a practical sense.

The long path of adopting had brought about circumstances that proved to be a culmination of the most suffering I had experienced — battling miscarriage, infertility, and secondary infertility, submitting to a call to love frozen orphans, then carrying them from suspension to glory. It had left me completely undone. Sin was no longer a list of things to do and not to do. It was not so easily divided. It was more than the question of heart intentions. Providence had illuminated parts of me to reveal that it is everywhere. It lived in my cells and even in my good works. I knew that in my resolve to love orphans, I stood condemned as it presented a life fully committed in obedience. Yet, in obedience, the death result of the fall was most near. Adoption was supposed to be life giving, but for me it had brought the deaths of my children. My response had left me feeling at odds with God. My worst fears had been realized. I also knew that I had done what I had been called to do. I knew of the other side for my little ones, and in it I rejoiced. God was caring for them through me, but it still hurt and I was not sure God was caring for me as well.

You might think it harsh to so associate sin with suffering. There is suffering without personal sin; however, suffering is always thrust upon us by the fall. The fall is a result of sin. It weaves its way into every space. This was exactly where God chose to reveal it in an undeniable way and show it as complicated and ugly as it is.

On the night I learned I had again given over my children to the Lord, to honor them in death, I wanted to say, "The Lord gives and the Lord takes away, blessed be the name of the Lord," but my heart was broken. The law of God and conviction of how life was supposed to be going down was clear in front of me. I knew I should be trusting in Him and His sovereign will. I should be laying down my rights and earthly possessions and following Him. I heard, like an echo, the scriptures well up within my soul with the should's and should-not's, and I knew I was failing.

I was angry that God would not allow me — and others — to see the faces of the children I had adopted. As a girl who knew her Bible, I knew that part of me was really bad. In my outward obedience, I had become like the ones Jesus rebuked the most — the Pharisees. This part of me was most difficult to own, yet was the most obvious. I knew it by my expectation for reciprocity, or good for the good I had done.

I had never seen myself as a woman at the well, a prostitute found faithful, or a murderous king. I had always felt that I really was a pretty good Christian. I had, for the most part, written myself out of all the parts of the Bible where a blatant sinner is lovingly confronted by the Savior. I had not identified with the desperation of the man who climbs high in a tree to get a glimpse of Jesus or the woman who stretches out for Jesus' garment, hoping for healing. If I am totally honest, I would not have understood even the concept of God's unsurpassed, far-reaching grace — the grace that had saved me — without the increase of the law in my life. That is the beauty of how God works. From the beginning, God gave me a Bible-taught aversion to a life characterized by drugs, extreme rebellion, facing social rejection, or coming apart at the seams. I could be a moralistic deist if necessary. He made me functional that way — until I began to understand the reach of the law. In this part of the story, it took me trying to do good and right things to see my need for Him and give Him a place to confront me with His perfect love.

Feeling so defeated by the things I hold true and right and suffering in a God-ordained way, how could I continue on? How was it that Job said, "Though he slay me, I will hope in him"?

Tim Keller expounds upon the extent the law meets me, even in the good things I may do.

> *What must we do, then, to be saved? To find God we must repent of the things we have done wrong, but if that is all you do, you may remain just an elder brother. To truly become a Christian we must also repent of the reasons we ever did anything right. Pharisees only repent of their sins, but Christians repent for the very roots of their righteousness, too. We must learn how to repent of the sin under all our other sins and under all our righteousness – the sin of seeking to be our own Savior and Lord. We must admit that we've put our ultimate hope in both our wrongdoing and right doing we have been seeking to get around God or get control of God in order to get hold of those things.*

> *It is only when you see the desire to be your own Savior and Lord—lying beneath both your sins and your moral goodness—that you are on the verge of becoming a Christian indeed. When you realize that the antidote to being bad is not just being good, you are on the brink. If you follow through, it will change everything—how you relate to God, self, others, the world, your work, you sins, your virtue. It's called the new birth because it's so radical. ~Tim Keller, The Prodigal God*

This was a moment when the above words made the most sense to me, even though I had been a believer in Jesus Christ for a long time. Wrestling with God with ordained pain, in and through a sure calling, forced a place of brutal honesty, even for a person well versed in right scriptures and appropriate applications. I realized I was the most unlike God I had known myself to be. My identity as a person who had been saved by Jesus was called into question in my soul. It was a complex mixture of a lot of things, both in and out of my control and even understandable given my circumstances — even circumstances judged noble — but I knew better. In the midst of this mess of real grief, despair, and knowledge of indwelling sin, I functionally wondered if God was still good and loved me. Knowing and wanting to do right yet failing, my soul began to speak aloud Romans 7:24-25 as the Bible began to read me:

> *So I find it to be a law that when I want to do right, evil lies close at hand. For I delight in the law of God, in my inner being, but I see in my members another law waging war against the law of my mind and making me captive to the law of sin that dwells in my members. Wretched man that I am! Who will deliver me from this body of death?*
>
> *So then, I myself serve the law of God with my mind, but with my flesh I serve the law of sin.*

James Montgomery Boice gives the argument that these words penned by Paul are indeed for a mature Christian as opposed to a person who is unsaved or even a "carnal Christian" (if such a person exists). He explains that "...sanctification is the process of coming increasingly to see how sinful we are so that we will depend constantly on Jesus Christ."[9]

God was making good on His promise to sanctify and the process seemed, even at the time, divinely designed. There was nowhere else to

---

[9] James Montgomery Boice, *An Expositional Commentary on Romans, vol. 2* (Baker Book House Company, 1992), 764 & 772.

turn, no other idea of how to obey. Parts of me were dying. For life, I must look to Jesus — not to me, but only to Him. The way I had previously understood the Christian life in terms of me and how well I was doing could not serve me any longer. When I was at my functional end and my soul was quieted, one sound remained. The sonorous voice that reverberates through history was singing over me. I needed that voice and those words. I needed the Old Story. It was Good News. It was the Gospel. It was not just for back then; it was (and it is) for now.

CHAPTER 10

At my follow-up appointment with my reproductive endocrinologist, we had talked about whether or not we would pursue a third adoption. There were no available embryos at the time. The staff had written letters to families who had discontinued paying for the storage of their remaining embryos, asking them to consider putting them up for adoption. It would be several weeks until they would hear back from them. This gave me time to heal and for Micah and me to decide if we could do this again. I still was inclined to run away — farther away – most of the time.

Something else happened. It is said that those whom God calls, He also equips. I have always been so very stubborn, to a fault. When Micah and I decided to adopt embryos, we thought that three transfers, or adoptions, seemed reasonable for us both financially and physically. After our first two adoptions, I was not sure I would be able to go through with our plan. My calling (and stubbornness worked into perseverance) kept overriding the uneasiness of my soul. In the back of my mind, I did not want to be in the elderly phase of life some day, rocking on a porch somewhere, wondering what might have happened. I was sure it would be a regret to not finish what I had begun. I am so Type A.

Well, it is mid-June. Our clinic suggested we call them to see if any families had relinquished their rights to their own embryos and made them available for adoption at this time. Honestly, I was very pessimistic. As I previously stated, the clinic had many embryos who had been abandoned and through letters from the staff, clients had been encouraged to choose to allow them to be given to other families or take responsibility for them themselves. Knowing they could choose to have them destroyed as another option, Micah and I had been praying they would choose life for their little ones, but were not sure many would respond that way.

Over the last couple of months, I have enjoyed the healing time. I have been reading a lot, particularly in the Psalms, adding in C.S. Lewis' A Grief Observed and I Will Carry You by Angie Smith. Valley of Vision continues to be a source of weighty truth. It hasn't been the most cheery of book line-ups, but indeed a help in pressing in to the call we have been given. Since our little ones now with Jesus don't share Micah's and my DNA, I see their faces in every culturally diverse place I go. I love the smiles of children, especially my own, shadowing the faces of those sharing eternity with the Son. There has been one question driving my relentless searching and grieving: Can I echo Job in saying, "Though He slay me [and may slay again], I will hope in Him"? Can I test this one more time? With adoring fear and supernatural fortitude, my answer is, "I am His." Please don't hear that as a boasting in my ability to hold myself in His hand, but rather a testimony of His saving grace. Now, the abundance of infinite strength to move forward at all is found only in the One who calls and supplies all our need according to the riches of Christ Jesus (Phil. 4:9).

Today, we met our third and final group of embryos. My initial call had revealed that the clinic had families respond to their letters and they asked that Micah and I come in as soon as possible. I was, at first, shocked and terrified. Then, remembering what I had asked — that God move in these families' hearts to choose life for their little ones — I felt humbled by His answer. As I stepped into the clinic I had so desired to run from a few months ago, the Lord brought Micah and I into hope. We sat down and were handed choices for our children, once again. There were two families with five remaining embryos. We chose two from one family that had been in storage since 2008. Then there was one remaining embryo from a family frozen back in 2004. I asked our nurse practitioner if we could please add this one and she did finally agree. Andrew and Elijah now have a sibling conceived in Andrew's birth year who will be younger than the both of them if God has that child to come and live with us :) It is amazing to us how after all this time, God has provided for these babies. It was such a tangible reminder that God never forgets or abandons. He is always working and willing on our behalf. I just pray one day I can share this precious truth with these children! Speaking of the little one frozen for 7 years, we were a bit concerned since the adopting family pays back storage fees, but our clinic staff was so kind and just added the one from 2004 into the mix of the others. Again, we are provided for.

So here we are, hearts bent on loving these frozen ones no matter the cost. We are beginning medication in about a week and if all goes as planned, they will be transferred on July 20. We know that God's plans for them will not be hindered. JIOJ ~ June 15, 2011

There were a few months between saying goodbye to our first adopted little ones and our third transfer. The first day of the medication cycle began on my birthday. By this time, I was a pro at following the schedule. As I posted the instructions up on the door of my bathroom linen closet, I knew it would be a guide less studied this time. Even though some days were repetitive, each day on the schedule took a shape all its own. It was like asking for daily bread — I knew what I needed to get through one day and I could not go beyond. I endured more of those dreaded shots, but I was afforded a bit more healing time from the last cycle.

The morning came to go to the procedure room. This could be the last and I knew that truth so well. It was almost as if realizations drew breaths and contracted muscles as I moved toward our little ones. I moved slowly, but moved nonetheless.

After our arrival and preparation, the embryologist came over and spoke with much guarded optimism. The first news to be shared was regarding our little '04 baby. He or she had not survived the thawing process and had been released from the void of waiting for so long. That little soul now rested with our others, now a total of eight, in the arms of Jesus. The thoughts of them all joining each other was a comfort. Again, I was reminded of the fragility of these tiny ones and the preciousness of life.

Yet amid sadness, I felt joy as the other two (first frozen in '08) looked "beautiful," quoting the embryologist. Earlier, she had made a slit in the outer shell called the zona pepellucida of the embryo. This procedure is called assisted hatching. It was even visible to Micah and me on the picture she provided, as we could see the beginnings of his or her emergence from the membrane.

There were so many prayers and thoughts swirling around this last transfer. I simply wanted to get it done and get home and toward the end of this wild, painful ride. In partial emotional numbness, I was ready to spend every moment I could with my little ones and accept the will of the One who brought me to them. I had to; I had no other choice.

The two-week wait was quiet and uneventful. I rested. My prayers were complex renderings of the woman I had become; a woman deeply wounded yet aware that somehow, I was loved. I had stopped trying to read Providence forward. I did have positive feelings sometimes followed by a tempering of reality, but did not allow myself to get too carried away with them.

A couple of mornings before my appointment to see results, I tested at home. I needed time to let what might be sink in. I again needed that protective space.

It was early, and Micah was not yet awake when I slipped out of bed and away to test. I have had many, many negative pregnancy tests in my life. I have had so many days when I was so sure I was pregnant, then crushed when the dye moved across the white space and only one line appeared. This was not one of those times.

The next day the line was darker. The next, even darker. I even got one of those digital tests so I could see the word "pregnant" all battery-operated and beautiful.

Before I knew it, I was back on that blessed sofa. I had officially tested upon my arrival at the doctor's office. On the other side of the closed door, I heard the nurse practitioner affirm what I already knew. "Finally!" she said to the gal completing the test. As she entered, her smile preceded her. Micah and I smiled (and cried), too.

CHAPTER 11

In beginning of August Micah had been asked to preach at the church where his father served as pastor in North Carolina. We enjoy visits to NC. The mountains are picturesque in the fall and always give me feelings of home. I know what all the doctors tell you about normal activity during pregnancy. I have no idea to this day what normal activity during pregnancy is supposed to be. Instead, I felt like I was carrying literal snowflakes; fragile and threatening to dissipate in my belly. Part of it, I confess, was worry and fear. Thinking back, I never wanted there to be anything I could pinpoint that I had done in negligence that may have resulted in anything bad. Sometimes I think my nurse practitioner was a better theologian than I during this time. "Whatever will happen, will happen," she would say. I wanted to make it happen; but again, I could not.

Then there was reckoning with the past. Something happens defensively when loss occurs. Pain of the emotional, mental kind cuts so deep the God-given part of my brain that controls self-preservation and protection of my little ones kicks into high gear. I remember starting to expect the very worst, even with good news. It was a constant struggle to remind myself what was really true and deal with the worst-case scenario for which I would involuntarily prepare.

It was a joy returning to family with good news. I think I spent the majority of the time trying to act normally (again, whatever normal is). It was such a joy to know someone, hopefully both someones, were growing and speak of them in the present tense as we visited for those few days.

The day we were to return home, just an hour before getting on the road, I began spotting. It was one of those moments I will never mistake for anything else. It felt like the life had been drained from me in one second. Here we go again. I spent just a moment leaning into the bathroom sink for support, asking God to prepare me for what was to come, assuming the very worst.

I simply did not know what to do for a bit. Taking the advice of Micah and my mother-in-law, who was available to watch the big boys, I went to the nearest emergency room. I was not sure that was the right decision, but I was not going to be able to get in the car and drive for a day if something was wrong that could be helped. When I sense something is wrong with my children instinct takes over, and something had to be wrong with a baby or babies. That is what all the books say anyway.

Micah and I arrived at the ER and I relayed the story of our embryo transfer to the triage nurse. She listened and was reluctant to say very much in response. It was out of desperation that I over-shared with whomever would listen. I had children in danger, and I was hoping to find a compassionate person to help. I was moved to a room. The nurse drew blood for an HCG (blood pregnancy test). Before the doctor did any kind of examination, I went for an ultrasound. I remember the room well. The gal performing the scan was very young. She and I talked at length about our adoption as she set up the equipment. She was careful not to be too promising about the information she could provide. Little did she know, I can read an ultrasound. The exam began and before a minute had passed, there were two little flashing white spots pulsing on the screen. I cannot even convey the joy I felt watching those two little spots. Micah stayed close. His thankful response only deepened our connectedness to those lives in the moment. Those were our two babies, growing, with heartbeats strong.

We were moved back to our ER room and the doctor came in soon thereafter. "Wow, twins!" he said. It was funny to hear. His smile was then dulled by the diagnosis, "Threatened Miscarriage." I like the sound of "twins" much better. By the time we walked out of the ER, everyone around had heard we were expecting twins... but we were in the emergency room with that smack-me-in-the-face diagnosis. Their smiles conveyed both kindness and concern as we walked past the nurses' station and out the sliding doors.

We went back to Micah's parents' home with the news that there were two babies still with us. I stabbed myself with another dose of IM progesterone with renewed vigor and we hit the road. If I could have, I would have announced our news to everyone from North Carolina to Kentucky.

We made it home and felt so thankful to God for continued life. With all the traveling, our family had yet to do anything to mark the occasion. Just down the road from our apartment was one of our favorite restaurants, and we decided to go out and eat, take a breath, and celebrate. We waited, sat down at our table, and ordered our food. In a second, my joy turned to complete stomach-sinking horror as I began bleeding profusely. Something had to be very wrong this time. I returned to the table only to dismiss myself to the parking lot where I called our nurse practitioner. The only thing she could offer me was an appointment in the office first thing Monday morning — and it was Saturday.

Micah and the boys escorted me home. At the nurse's admonition, I tried to lie as quietly as possible. The only movement I could not get under control fell within the hours I spent sobbing.

It felt like God had multiplied my joy and then, with impending sorrow, multiplied my grief. I rambled for the better part of the day with Micah close at my side. I would sway between guilt, fear, and outright anger. It was here that I continued learning a most difficult lesson. I kept trying to disguise pain with faith language. There was something Micah had said early on in my sufferings and the truth behind it was my temporal salvation: Crying out to God with whatever I am thinking and feeling is an act of faith. So often I want to clean myself up and fashion the external to what makes me feel more faithful. He knows it all anyway and simply says, "Come." Jesus is faithful and I am in Him and in His incarnation, He knows my frailty. That was the day for me, in pain and sheer desperation. I again landed before the throne in a heap. All the things I desired, I prayed. All the things I feared, I confessed. All the things I just did not understand, I said in vulnerability. The most astounding thing: God never turned away from me. Not once. He may have felt distant for the moment, but behind His mysterious providence was a smiling face. He did not smile without entering into the pain, but thank goodness His nature was not affected by it. Someone had to be the steady one.

Monday morning, Micah and I made the trip in to the doctor. I was thankful that they took me even earlier than I thought would be possible.

I knew the drill. He and I sat eagerly in the waiting room and were taken back fairly quickly. I know I had a look of exhaustion when the nurse took my vital signs and listened to the details of our previous ER visit in North Carolina. She had a kind look of hopefulness in her eyes. This was the same nurse who had vowed to pray after each of our transfers. Her calmness was a welcomed energy. I needed others to be hopeful for me, so her presence fit the bill. We went into the exam room and prepared for another ultrasound. The nurse practitioner came in and, with a sigh, quickly began looking for little heartbeats. She very swiftly found them. It was just seconds. Then she said the oddest thing. I can still hear the words ringing in my ears. At first, I thought something was terribly wrong. "I can't believe they didn't see this in the ER," she said with a matter-of-fact disposition.

"See what?" I asked.

Then, she began to count. There are times and places you expect to hear counting. Counting sheep, apples for a cobbler, to ten, in an attempt to find self-control...during an ultrasound is not one of those. "One, two, three," she said. "Three babies." Three heartbeats.

All that would come out of my mouth was the phrase, "You're joking." I think I said it several times. She was not joking. I looked over at my sweet, supportive husband and he was staring at the floor, his eyes wide and face fixed.

For the next few minutes, our NP determined which babies shared a sac. One of our embryos had split into two babies and therefore were identical, mono-chorionic, di-amniotic twins. The other embryo had indeed survived and was growing in his or her own sac. There is a 1 in 10,000 chance of this happening. The bleeding was attributed to me carrying three babies at one time. It was putting a strain on my cervix, but it was superficial and did not seem to be a threat. After many congratulations, Micah and I walked out of that room completely turned upside down. I could not even think straight. It was such a mixture of joy and complete shock. In my fertility lifetime of suffering and intervention, God had not given me the gift of a surprise pregnancy. Instead, this was my surprise. As we left the office, everyone we passed already knew we were going to have three babies. They were all so calm and so excited. I was freaking out — in a good way.

The car ride home was filled with calls to family and close friends with the preface, "Are you sitting down?" I arrived home, where my friend Jaime was taking care of my big boys. She came over to the car after we pulled in with a concerned look on her face. Her demeanor quickly turned to elation when I explained what had happened at the doctor's office. I think that sums up my first week as a woman carrying triplets. I was astounded, as were others.

CHAPTER 12

From the very beginning, I knew this pregnancy would be different than the ones I had experienced before. Many things I read in pregnancy books just did not apply anymore. Micah did purchase a multiples pregnancy book and it was somewhat helpful. It was simplistically educational, labeling complications without diagnosis, and I appreciated the special attention given to the topics experienced by mothers of multiples. One thing it assuredly did, in addition to providing information, was make me completely insane.

One of the things in the book and, well, everywhere else I turned, was information regarding the threatening capabilities with the presence of spotting. The initial spotting I experienced in North Carolina continued for the first nine weeks. I called the doctor's office at least once a week questioning the normalcy of what my body was doing. I was afraid to move. If I did too much, it seemed to make it worse. Our medical overseer, still our nurse practitioner, kept reminding me (one who has studied God's Sovereignty at length) that whatever would happen, will happen (so very true — still, not so reassuring). I decided if all I could do, even in my own estimation, was lie still then I would, and I did. Micah and I had an L-shaped sofa at the time, and the spot in the corner became ideal for keeping my quickly-expanding belly propped up. Being on the couch also gave me the ability to stay in the living room with my family. I did go out of the house some and try to act normal, and not like I was growing three babies simultaneously. Some people would ask about my pregnancy. The minute "triplets" or "three" left my mouth, theirs dropped open and we no longer had eye contact. They just kept staring at my belly. Regardless of the outing, being conscious of how much I was moving was constantly looming over every activity.

After all I had been through — years of fertility issues and then the loss of so many little ones — there was a part of me that still expected the worst. That was the most difficult part. In my defensiveness, expecting something terrible to happen in theory promised to cushion the blow of what was actually happening, whatever it might be. Again, having read God's words about thinking on what is true and fervently praying for the miraculous seemed like asking for heartbreak, given my protective posture. On the other side of things, I honestly wanted to enjoy every moment of each beating heart strengthening daily in my womb. I knew the days had been short with our other little ones and I knew how very much I missed them once it was confirmed they were no longer with me. The realist in me knew they might not stay with me long. Another part, who longed to see the path of angels unaware, knew if God was for them living and growing, it would be accomplished. I had loved and lost, and that had changed my capacity and knowledge of the cost of loving. I also marveled at the gift of these three little ones. From the minute I knew of them, I had been dreaming of their faces and thinking of their futures. I wanted so much to meet these three and have the opportunity to hold them.

One of the very first things Micah did when he found out we were expecting triplets was Google "triplets" and look at pictures of women fully blossomed in multiple pregnancy bliss. He came in one afternoon with a, "Hey! Look at this!" and proceeded to show me the images he had found on the internet. That was so very kind of him (is there a font for sarcasm?)! Men and women are so very different in the ways they prepare for situations like this. Of all his multiple-pregnancy-dad-epiphanies, one was deciding that while he may have considered a tummy tuck un-frugal and borderline un-godly before, after seeing those pictures, it may be ungodly to not afford me a post-pregnancy procedure. As I contemplated the way my body could change, I looked at my short waist and wonder where in the world everyone was going to fit.

So day-by-day, the babies grew and I grew. After ultrasounds and continued monitoring up to nine weeks gestation, we graduated to a perinatologist, or high-risk obstetrician. The threatening symptoms proved to be a continuing part of my pregnancy with the babies. It was something that, despite information that would suggest otherwise, was completely normal. Leaving behind beloved, familiar medical professionals, it was so very important to me that we find a doctor who had much experience in the delivery of multiples. Our reproductive endocrinologist's office had given us a referral and since we trusted them, I trusted their recommendation. The new office was on another floor of the same building as the RE. This particular doctor would also prove to be a gift from God.

On our first visit, we met Dr. Bill Koontz in his private office. To the left of the door was a corkboard full of sets of twins, triplets, and quintuplets. He was calm, witty, and hit it off with Micah almost immediately. They both have a mutual love for history, and his story-telling ability was endearing, but was he capable of bringing our precious little ones into the world? As the conversation drew to the end of the salutary, initial formalities, we got down to business. Everything he mentioned as being a concern in multiple, high-risk pregnancies were things I was familiar with to some degree, due to the books I had been reading. His knowledge base came through in his explanations, and his caution showed wisdom built by many years of practice (both struggles and successes). He also spoke in a way that I could understand and that was indispensible. The last and most concerning complication he mentioned was Twin-To-Twin Transfusion Syndrome.

The internet can prove to be a blessing and a curse, as one can find just about any information supporting any theory or concern ad nauseum. The first evening I perused YouTube with "triplets" in the search engine, I came across multiple videos both informational and testimonial with the heading "TTTS." The first I clicked on was a memorial for two little boys lost to TTTS early in a twin pregnancy. I was moved to tears. Fear gripped my heart as I watched, and I turned it off after a minute or so. I was curious though. The next recommended videos originated from a hospital in Philadelphia. They were a nine-part informational piece regarding all medical aspects of the disease and possible treatments. I have a bit of a medical background and I found the information fascinating. The books I had gave very little information. I did arm myself with enough knowledge to have an intelligent conversation about it, but I left it behind praying we would never encounter such a problem.

Hearing our doctor speak about TTTS was reassuring in that he was aware of its potential and would watch for it from the beginning. He was also quick to share his plan, should a plan be needed to address it. I loved that about him. He was ready and willing to seek outside help. On the other hand, I had wished it really was not as bad as the information I had already heard. From his level of seriousness, I was sure that it was a real concern and he would be on the lookout for the signs.

Micah and I left the office feeling encouraged. God had gone before us in that appointment and we were both glad to feel as if he was meeting our mortal needs in supernatural and very practical ways.

I was thinking this morning, going over all the information we received in my head, that as believers in a Sovereign God, there is no possible "what if..." that is out of His plan; no surprises or twists of fate. Knowing myself as I do, having a heavenly perspective beyond my earthly view is a must for times like these. My desire and prayer in an attempt to walk by faith and not by sight through this season is to feel God's invisible hand even more so than I feel all the visible ones supporting me over the next months. And thankfully, even when my faith is small and I get bogged down looking at the mountain ahead, God's hand is not diminished. He, being the object of faith, bears the weight. And even more intimately, His hands and arms are carrying us along (Isaiah 40:11), close to His heart. I can't imagine a better place to rest in the course of uncertainty. JIOJ ~ September 17, 2011

We got to know Dr. Koontz very well. I saw him often. He and Micah talked about Chick-fil-a, history, and other things. I learned that he loves to scuba dive and heard about his grandchildren. He even shared pictures as he described what he loved about each of them. Loving children is a quality most highly desired in the person who would be delivering mine. For nine weeks, we got to know one another and things moved forward smoothly. As the babies grew, we began to see differences in them that hinted at their personalities. They began to move around. I could feel different movements from each baby.

The days passed, until the day we learned more details about who I would have the pleasure of meeting. I had never waited to find out gender and I was not going to begin now!

The conversations and situations that led up to this point are so clear in my mind.

A long time ago, I had heard the name Eliana and its meaning: "God answered," or "God responded." A few years ago, Micah brought home a pair of the cutest brown Mary Janes that had been left in the Chick-fil-A lost-and-found for months and months. Of course we had no girls at the time, but I held on to them and wondered if we would ever have an Eliana to fill them. I am good at sharing things we don't need or use, but for some reason, these shoes have stayed with me along with the name.

In the week that followed our big news — that God had given us triplets — Micah reminded me of a girl name, Isabella, that he and I had talked about even before Andrew was born. From the minute he said it, it seemed to be a no brainer. I hadn't imagined that God might give us two girls and I loved the names together — especially for twins.

The funny thing is, we haven't had the most successful collaboration when discussing boy names. We would have very spirited conversations over Micah's choices (he really likes unique names from deceased presidents and theologians) and my lack of any alternatives. The week I found out I was expecting, I read a devotion about Sarah and Isaac. When we found out about the three babies we, like Sarah, did a lot of laughing. Micah's mother immediately suggested Isaac right from the beginning. It made perfect sense. If there was a boy who needed a name, that one would fit.

Beyond these, we had no other names. I bought a book of 10,000 baby names, but it was no help at all. Of course, if the Lord had differently for us, we could have adjusted. But I wondered if He had provided us the names of our children even before we knew their genders.

So yesterday, Micah and I went to our appointment. I looked at Micah as he dropped me off at the office door and said, "Let's go see if these babies are who we think they are!" At this point, you may think I am crazy. That's okay. There are many days I feel completely crazy! Through this whole process, I have been impressed over and over to trust God's care and sovereignty. I have spoken out for frozen lives whose days are numbered even before they are a thought in human existence. I firmly believe that God just doesn't create people, but souls that show His providence throughout history. Psalm 139:16 says, "Your eyes saw my unformed substance; in your book were written, every one of them, the days that were formed for me, when as yet there was none of them." We are all not here together by chance, friends. When I have thought about names, it has been more about learning who these individuals already are rather than who they will become.

So there we are, in the ultrasound room, watching the screen. Baby A is first; the singleton. Everything looks good... and clearly, it's a boy! "There's Isaac!" I said to Micah.

"What if they are all boys?!?" he replied. I knew that the iden-tical ones would be the same gender, so another boy would guarantee all boys.

"Five boys!" I exclaimed. The ultrasound tech laughed and said she was then scared to look at the other two babies :) Baby B was the most difficult to see, so she moved to Baby C. It seemed like it took a while to find the right angle and check all the important stuff. Then, it was clear. The UT grabbed my arm. "It's a girl!" she said with a smile. For the next few minutes I tried to focus on the screen with teary eyes. Baby B confirmed it. There they were; Eliana and Isabella. JIOJ ~ Oct. 15, 2011

It was at this appointment that Dr. K. first mentioned TTTS as a pos-sible issue for our babies, particularly the girls. We had known from very early on that the girls were identical and that they shared a blood supply since they shared a singular placenta or chorion. They did not share an amnion, however, as they did not share amniotic fluid. In Twin-to-Twin Transfusion Syndrome, there is unequal sharing of the placenta. One baby (the recipient) gets an over-abundance of the blood supply and the other baby (the donor) does not get enough. This causes many problems for both babies. Many times the recipient suffers polyhydramnios, or an excess of amniotic fluid, and may develop hydrops or collections of fluid, usu-ally due to cardiac issues. The donor's growth is impeded as blood supply is inadequate, and therefore nutrients are in short supply. The result is decreased amniotic fluid, as it also affects kidney function.

With the assistance of the Fetal Care Center in Cincinnati, a segment of Cincinnati Children's Hospital and a leader in the treatment of TTTS, our doctor did not give our babies a TTTS diagnosis at this time. He was committed to watch them closely for worsening of symptoms, as things can change quickly.

Dr. K. was intent on watching for TTTS. Knowing it could be on the horizon, I reluctantly went back to the internet. It was the most helpful source since there was very little in the pregnancy books on my shelf regarding this syndrome. What I found was completely and utterly heart breaking. The statistic I remember reading that bounced off the walls of my brain was that 90-100% of babies affected early in gestation by TTTS die if it is left untreated. Despair does not begin to describe what I felt trying to swallow those numbers. I am typically a person who does not leave a stone unturned and as frightening as the scenarios I read about, I barreled through all the information I could. I searched and searched, determined to be as informed as possible.

Early on, we had seen some size discordance in the girls. No one worried too much about it at first, but at around 15 weeks, their sizes were more significantly different. After the difference was communicated to our doctor, he suggested a follow-up ultrasound in a little over two weeks.

This ultrasound was much different than the ones we had experienced before. The room was different, the technician was different, and the atmosphere was astronomically different. In the first few moments, I again marveled at the number of limbs, bellies, and heads on the screen. The gal began measuring the babies. She started with baby A, Isaac. She took values for head circumference, fluid level, looked for a visible bladder, and measured the blood flow in each umbilical cord. By this time, I had read enough that I knew what to look for, too. She then tried to gather the same information for Eliana, but with no success. She moved to Isabella, then back to Eliana. The differences were clear. Within hours, we were referred to the Fetal Care Center in Cincinnati, Ohio.

We got to see our little ones today. I listened to a song by Out of the Grey before I went into the doctor's office called "Brave." It reminded me that before Micah and I even walked into the ultrasound room, God would be there. He was waiting, and had been there all along. As we arrived, settled in, and watched the monitor, I once again thought, He has gone before us. We saw our three kicking, squiggling, punching little babies. Seeing their little hands and feet made me smile. Then, when the US Tech panned down to Eliana and did confirm that her amniotic fluid level is quite decreased and that she is still significantly smaller, I really needed that truth. As I cried throughout the rest of the US, seeing each one of them thriving yet unaware of the danger ahead, I had to believe that truth.

So what we had prayed for — that God would keep our twins from TTTS — He has answered differently than we had wanted. It seems at this point, they do have Stage 1. Our doc immediately called the Fetal Care Center in Cincinnati and by this afternoon, we were scheduled to have several tests this coming Tuesday and Wednesday. The nurse with whom I spoke was very kind and compassionate and assured me that by Wednesday afternoon, we will have their recommendations for caring for our babies. There aren't many things they can do to treat TTTS, but one fairly effective, cutting edge treatment is Fetal Laser Surgery. If the specialists recommend this for us, we would go ahead with it on Thursday.

As you can imagine, we are extremely needy right now. I am going to be following the example of those parents in Luke 15, bringing my babies to Jesus that He might touch them. I ask that you do the same on their behalf. TTTS is a scary disease, but I know that Jesus is able to heal them. He may choose to use the doctors in Cincinnati, so please pray for each of them. We also desire prayer for the boys, as they are with different care-givers. For Micah and myself, I ask that each one of you hold God to His word; that His power is made perfect in our weakness. Even though this road is scary, He continues to go before and will carry us though whatever lies ahead. ~JIOJ, November 4, 2011

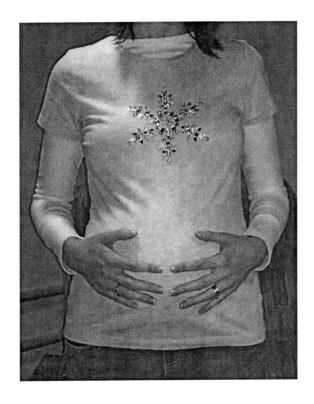

CHAPTER 13

There is some music that is very good for traveling. The evening before my appointments, after the boys were dropped off and well taken care of, Micah and I headed toward Cincinnati. We had just picked up the new Coldplay CD and in our fuel efficient, road hugging Ford Fit, we moved through the rolling hills of Kentucky.

I remember clearly not liking Mylo Xyloto[10] so much, before I realized how well it propelled us toward uncertainty. The song "Paradise" was reflective. If the music selection was much more orthodox, it would cause me to sob uncontrollably or become so inwardly focused on how I was handling the suffering, I would become despondent. I guess I have never thought much about battle chants, but in these moments, I completely understood their use. There are times an old adage is not so foreign and makes one appreciate the author. "Ignorance is Bliss" was one that resonated through our travel as I held babies in my belly, aware of a possible difficult diagnosis, so desiring bliss. I wanted to know, but then again, I did not. I knew better, so we traveled on. Micah and I were both quiet most of the trip.

---

[10] Coldplay, *Mylo Xyloto* (Parlophone Records, Ltd., 2011).

Our first visit, we spent the night in a nearby hotel to make certain we could arrive at the hospital early the next morning. We had a suite at the end of the building. The room was lovely but the bed was too soft and it took four pillows to prop everyone up while I attempted to pray and confess away fear, not think about all that I was thinking about, and sleep. After a restless night, we awoke early and headed toward the Cincinnati Children's Hospital. It was a place neither Micah nor I had been before and we were thankful for GPS as we braved a frigid morning. Getting lost would have only added to my anxiety. I did not want another stressor to add to the resounding pounding in my heart and continuing list of questions I was replaying in my brain.

We escaped the chill into the brightly colored main building among other sprawled medical buildings in the middle of city blocks. After we got our bearings, we headed to our first appointment. We settled in for the day among the little and larger patients darting through the hallways and sitting waiting in the areas equipped with video games and TVs playing cartoons.

After a 1.5 hour MRI, 3 hour ultrasound, and another 1 hour fetal echo cardiogram for each baby, we did sit down with the team at the Fetal Care Center in Cincinnati yesterday. First of all, I want to say that this experience has been amazing. We had the ability to watch our babies for hours. Isaac loves to kick and punch and wave. He is growing very well and likes to try to get in all the pictures of his sisters. It is almost like he knows what the docs want to see at any given moment and tries to hide that particular body part from them as long as he can. Eliana can move from one side of my belly to the other in just a few minutes, trying to avoid pictures :) Isabella likes to straighten her legs out as far as they can go. There were times when she and Eliana would lay chest to chest and you could see their beating hearts in a single image. We watched them count their fingers and toes, measure bones in their bodies, multiple parts of their brains and bellies, isolate their tiny veins, arteries, and heart valves, and do studies on their blood flow, etc. They are — we are — fearfully and wonderfully made. And the way God has gifted us to be able to see these kinds of things and get to know our babies even now is so very gracious of Him.

The Maternal-Fetal Medicine Doctor did another quick scan of the babies to show us what exactly he wanted to talk with us about and then gave his recommendations. Instead of just one this-is-what-it-is-and-this-is-what-we-do answer, he gave us several things to weigh. First of all, the girls do indeed have TTTS. He commended our doctor here in Louisville for sending us to Cincinnati so quickly because the girls are in the beginning stages. There is a significant size difference in the girls as well as in their amniotic fluid levels but those things alone do not show enough of a discrepancy to warrant a full diagnosis in and of themselves. However, in Isabella (known as the recipient twin), there is some mild thickening in her heart and some hypertension. Cardiac changes in any of the babies are a big concern. Although the doctor feels that surgery is more than likely inevitable, there are a couple of reasons to wait a bit. First of all, our sweet Isaac is guarding the entry point of where they would need to go in to sever the blood vessels between the girls. It would be a big risk to him to go in at this point. Also, I have a history of preterm labor and most women deliver within 70 days after the surgery. I am 19 weeks this week, so waiting is ideal since the girls are still in the early stages.

In order to treat the hypertension in Isabella and alleviate some stress on her heart, I am taking blood pressure medication. Since TTTS can move quickly, they are repeating the ultrasound and fetal echo on Monday.

*Throughout this pregnancy, I have found myself realizing that indeed I need Thee every hour. God has been teaching me to pray, "Give us this day our daily bread," and to be thankful for each moment instead of taking this day for granted and trying to see way down the road. I think this is where we are left today; in **conscious dependence on God** for each breath, each step forward, and only one day at a time. The truth is, this is where we all live every day. The **consciousness** part is a gift.*

However, I do not and will not do this perfectly and I do not have to. During the MRI, the gal told me in the beginning it would take around an hour to complete. Micah was allowed in the room with me but because of the loudness of the machine, we wouldn't be able to talk. I was disappointed that he couldn't even read to me, as he and I are both reading a new book together. She brought out a box of DVDs for me to choose from so I could watch a movie on goggles while in the machine. I looked through the box and just didn't feel that watching Hannah Montana, Transformers, or some romantic comedy would feel appropriate. The gal then offered some music and headphones. I thought those would help drown out the machine and give me a nice backdrop to be still and pray for the babies. Isaiah 40:11 has been a verse I have meditated on during tough days and wanted so much to have a moment to remember how Jesus carries me in His arms while I lay in this noisy tube. Little did I know, the "soft" station she chose filled my ears with George Michael's "Father Figure," Katy Perry's "Hot N Cold," and Elton John's "Bennie and the Jets," just to name a few. The "spiritualness" just wasn't happening... on my part anyway. But Jesus loving me and interceding for me never ceased. This is not up to me or about me. It is about what He has done and continues to do. I am fully and completely dependent on Him and He is able. ~JIOJ, November 10, 2011

It felt as though we were in the best physical hands possible. We appreciated that someone, somewhere was equipped with the knowledge to help us. The staff's kindness and hospitality were an added comfort. The Center itself was designed to be a haven for people suffering through various serious complications affecting their unborn children. This place housed those marked by concern and when weeping prevailed, despite the anonymity, it was palpable. There was also a lot of privacy in the segments of conference rooms, waiting rooms, offices, and the two more typical hospital rooms for patients post fetal laser surgery. The nature of the unit leant itself to the precarious nature of the problems it was designed to treat. There was something very life-affirming about this place where doctors and nurses labored to take attentive care of the not-yet-born patients and the mothers and fathers who loved them so.

Even before leaving from our first visit, our second had been scheduled within a few days. TTTS can become more complicated very quickly and time between visits reflected that fact. We would be watching some areas of concern very closely. Eliana, our donor, was hanging in there, still measuring small with very little amniotic fluid but sporting a visible bladder and moving around like a champ. Isabella was the recipient and became the most concerning. In those first two visits, there were measurable signs of increasing stress on her heart. The doctor's recommendation was to give me Procardia, a blood pressure medication that enters the placenta, in an attempt to reduce the pressure the extra blood supply was adding to Bella's heart. We were still given the advice to continue to wait, given the difficulty of fetal laser surgery and the possibility of losing all the babies.

After the first two visits, we waited one week. You may picture time here as a thorny, slow moving, slimy snail if such a creature exists.

The visit following (our third), we again sat for hours watching our babies flutter and stretch on the monitor of the high-tech ultrasound screens. By this time, the technicians were getting to know us all very well and even began calling the babies by name. We were getting to know them also. After another day of tests, Micah and I found ourselves back in the very private waiting room. By this time, I was thankful for the recliner as my pregnant condition was making most other non-reclining positions quite uncomfortable. Isabella's results came back worse than before. I was diagnosed with TTTS Stage IIIC, due to her severe cardiomyopathy. There are fives stages in TTTS. Beyond our current stage, hydrops occur due to heart failure, Stage 4. Stage 5 is death. The facts made me physically ill.

Isabella was clearly struggling so much, along with our fighting-for-nutrients Ellie girl. I wanted someone to do something more. We had another conversation and another scan to see if there was any route adjacent to the affected blood vessels where the doc could safely enter the girls' placenta without compromising Isaac's. With no clear path without great risk to be found, the doctors still suggested we put off surgery. The choice was so hard — almost too much for a mama to bear without feeling as if I was choosing one child over another. I leaned heavily on the doctors and Micah to help me wait.

CHAPTER 14

And the Lord will fight for you, and you have only to be silent. Exodus 14:14

Every day was a battle. Back home, I would wake up after a restless night, remember where I was, where the babies were, hear the boys bouncing around our apartment, and feel the knot in my stomach again. What would this day bring? What do you do when thinking on things that are true reveal terrifying realities? The overwhelming nature of constant suspense sent me into emotional overload.

It was in this space that I understood groanings too deep for words. Years before, I did a Bible study through the book of Hebrews. In its pages, God gave me hope for each day when faith talk and right attitudes were elusive.

> *Now the point in what we are saying is this: we have such a high priest, one who is seated at the right hand of the throne of the Majesty in heaven, a minister in the holy places, in the true tent that the Lord set up, not man. Hebrews 8:1-2*

> *Consequently, he is able to save to the uttermost those who draw near to God through him, since he always lives to make intercession for them. Hebrews 7:25*

Having blurted out every known request a thousand times, I would close my eyes and pray for faith to believe that the throne room exists just as it is written: God in the center, Jesus at His right hand praying for me, the Holy Spirit interceding on my behalf. Sometimes, God would bring to my mind the scriptures that tell me I have been seated with Christ at the right hand of God and I would feel so thankful that when I opened my eyes in a world of uncertainty, part of my soul would still remain there in complete security. God did grant me belief and yet I did not believe perfectly, as evidenced by my continued anxieties. Trying to apply verses about not being anxious became anxiety producing. Some days, I would just lie there. Other days when doctor appointments required me to move, I prayed for Jesus to pick me up and carry me. Again, Isaiah 40:11 says, "He tends His flock like a Shepherd. He gathers the lambs in His arms and carries them close to His heart. He gently leads those who have young." I inwardly and outwardly needed my Shepherd.

In the years prior, I had read and re-read the story of the man who came to Jesus with his son who was demon possessed. There are aspects of this account that so resonated with my soul. I had recounted it a number of times. The other disciples had failed to deliver this boy from this terrible oppression and Jesus received him. The man asked Jesus for help and compassion. Jesus replied, "All things are possible for one who believes." The man did not pipe up with verbal surety of belief without angst but in safe-self-awareness, he confessed directly to the God-Man Jesus Christ, "I believe, help my unbelief."

It seems an important time to get it right — when my babies are ill and I need a Healer.

I could not fix or give a façade to the parts of me still unredeemed that manifested unbelief to make them appear anything different than what they were. I knew that when called to be perfect as my Father in heaven is perfect in praying for the precious souls living inside of me, sick with a disease that might easily kill them, inward focus was futile. It was the blessing of the knowledge of my unbelief that made me aware that I was no longer in the position to use the strength of my faith as a means to negotiate a good outcome. I was forced to rest in the object of my faith — the One found faithful, Jesus Christ. I am His because He has made me His. I cannot mess it up because He does not mess up.

The knowledge that Jesus came to rescue all types of sinners seeped its way a little deeper into my soul. There was no point of profound discovery but slowly, as God continued to love me, to draw me to Him, I knew it was in the confessing my unbelief and trusting in Jesus's perfect life lived for me that I could go from day to night to day.

For those of you interested in my treatment for TTTS, the only thing I did besides bed rest and take Procardia was drink protein shakes. There were two reasons I downed those nasty things. First, I had read that they might help. One of the most influential doctors in the United States committed to treating TTTS always suggests that his patients drink these shakes to help balance the excess water weight and low blood protein levels. Second, I was not able to meet the suggested caloric intake for a gal growing three babies due to my stomach's ascent into my lungs and the severe nausea that accompanied me through most of my pregnancy. I knew that even though the shakes tasted like pureed chocolate meat, they would be a great resource for nutrition. I drank two or three a day by gulping them through a straw at the back of my throat, completely bypassing my taste buds.

Right before Thanksgiving, we arrived at our fourth visit to the Fetal Care Center. All the testing gave us the encouragement that the medication was beginning to help sweet Isabella. The numbers that provided information corresponding to the way her little heart was being affected by TTTS showed some improvement. It was such a deep relief. Isaac and Eliana kept the status quo.

Back and forth we traveled.

Many couples go to the Fetal Care Center, receive treatment, and either move to the Ante-Partum floor or return home. We were a different case. Every week, we went through testing, met with the doctor in the stillness of the private wing, and again went home to wait. There was absolutely nothing familiar in Cincinnati with the exception of the hospital and the hotel. Before these trips, I had only been to this city a handful of times. Even though the bed in our first-booked-suite was uncomfortable, when we had to stay overnight at the discounted hotel for hospital patients, I asked for the same room every consecutive trip. Familiarity was a comfort.

Some visits, my medication was adjusted to suit Isabella's needs and other weeks it was simply maintained as we continued to watch the babies. At the same time, I was monitored for all the normal stuff in Louisville. Both groups of staff became like family. In all that time, Micah and I learned to navigate each hospital. I found favorite snacks in the respective cafeterias. Micah learned to drive me around in a wheelchair like a champ. He zoomed through the hallways of Cincinnati Children's, playfully finding something recreational for us to do together.

Andrew and Elijah learned to lean on friends of ours for care, good food, and kind company. I learned to lean on other caregivers for our boys too when I was not physically able to be there for them. As a mom who is used to having her kiddos around all the time, this was different. Mr. Bruce and Mrs. Tana's house was a great place for them to be. It was always reported to be full of great food and fun video games. It made the multiple trips to Ohio tolerable, knowing they were in such capable hands.

In those bed rest weeks, I experienced love from others in a new way. I have always been a person that generally wants to help. Since I was essentially incapacitated, people from our church home began coming over weekly to help with chores, take the big boys on outings, and bring meals. I would have never had the opportunity otherwise to get to know such sweet individuals and families. Other friends jumped in to help as well. As women entered our home, fed us delicious food, and spent time so kindly folding socks, tidying up dishes, and taking on whatever else was on the to do list, bonds were formed. When someone lovingly folds your unmentionables, it just happens. I was in a very vulnerable state. I could not do anything as much as I desired.

So much in life feels so very unique to our own, complicated circumstances. It can be very isolating; the feeling that no one else understands. What is ironic is that even as seemingly different the story God was writing in my life, the isolation and loneliness is congruent with most persons en masse. During my pregnancy with the triplets most especially, I felt very alone in the circumstances of day-to-day, treading forward into uncertainty. I remember praying that God would reveal Himself to me in ways I could feel.

As days turned to weeks and weeks into months, there was a stirring of a large group of people — not necessarily a singular group but collectively from different places reaching me — that entered into our lives through prayer. Information about the triplets' and my needs was provided by both internet and word of mouth and the result was a construct of support. Those in this group allowed their hearts to be drawn in a heavenward direction through intercession. Our family blog was the place we gave public information and received the most precious words. Emails and messages came weekly. Churches added us to their prayer lists. I even received a blanket quilted by a women's prayer group from my aunt's church in Winston Salem, NC. When I received it in the mail, I remember touching the hand-tied quilt, imagining the hands securing the seams. There were so many praying. It was moving to know that others were carrying my babies and me to the throne of our Father. I know the days I received emails, calls, or even blog comments ministered to me in ways that whispered a direct answer to my prayers for felt encouragements.

Week after week.... Ultrasound after ultrasound.... Long wait after long wait... home again for bed rest... until the milestone of twenty-six weeks. With each one of the babies stable, there was a glimmer of hope on the horizon that they all might remain with us until birth. The day finally came when I officially graduated from The Fetal Care Center. From the doctor's perspective, babies affected by TTTS should be delivered after twenty-six weeks gestation, as the risks of prematurity as a neonate decrease. We were patients at Cincinnati Children's Hospital for eight long weeks. On our final visit, it was confirmed to us what a miracle it was that we had made it so far. All our babies were alive with no surgical intervention. One doctor went as far as to disclose his negative prognosis for us in the beginning. He was pleasantly surprised by the end of our time with him. As Micah and I dared to continue to hope, we thanked God for each of the staff and for the continued life of our babies. With pictures of he and me with the staff stored on our cell phones and plenty of well wishes, we drove I-71 south from Cincinnati for a final time with all babies still inside.

Our first visit in Louisville after our FCC graduation, Dr. Koontz was visibly, pleasantly surprised upon my return with his three other patients. I remembered his countenance when he had first sent us to Cincinnati. He had not been happy at all, and it was perceivable despite his attempt to be professional. In cautious celebration, I began to further progress on the final leg of my triplet pregnancy in the weeks of waiting for delivery.

It was all smooth sailing... Not.

I frequented the larger rooms (suitable for the extra monitor for third babies) in the triage department of labor and delivery during the multiple trips I made over the next weeks. I could have run the reception desk without batting an eye after donning ID bracelets and signing those HIPPA forms (as well as every other electronic form) over and over again. One of the visits resulted from dehydration in the height of Norovirus season. This caused contractions and much distress. I have never been more thankful for an IV as I was that evening. I received much needed fluids and anti-nausea medication. I also was given a speedy introduction to medications used to stop labor, as dehydration will cause contractions. Those meds were brutal but I was so thankful that as long as the babies were well, I could have assistance with keeping them inside as long as possible.

At the end of January, I went to the hospital with more contractions. By this time, I was a big ol' girl. I was already well past my largest with my previous two pregnancies both in size and weight. The strain on my body was apparent. Knowing when the strain of carrying three babies was affecting the progression of labor from home was not so easy to discern. When I did arrive back at the hospital this particular January evening, I was contracting more than my doc was comfortable with and he quickly ordered more medication to stop it. With forward progression, steroid shots were ordered to move along lung development in the babies. I was admitted to the hospital for observation while the two shots were administered over a weekend. It was a Friday. I would see my doc again on Monday in his office, in an adjacent building to my room.

My prayer was for the answer to be clear. A part of me was anxious to be home, as I missed being with Andrew and Elijah terribly. Another part liked the knowledge that I had access to care around the clock in the hospital. Sometimes the right thing to do is elusive. Sometimes it is clear.

When Dr. Koontz checked to see how well I had handled the steroids, I had moved even farther down the labor road. It was crystal clear I needed to remain at the hospital until the babies were delivered.

Micah's parents came in to town to take care of the boys so he could spend evenings with me in the hospital. Even in a few days, I progressed in size to the point of not being able to breathe when lying horizontally (which still appeared to be propped up to everyone else). We had a few visitors. I learned to pass the time knitting, thanks to some traveling knitting teachers, and reading. Doing things that were tedious, like knitting little hats for three tiny heads, was calming. I did some writing. Mostly, it was quiet.

I was getting pretty discouraged at the beginning of this past week. Just not sure how much longer — for the babies' sake and mine. I was again trying to read Providence forward, which is impossible. What, when, how, and why were constantly on my mind. Once again, Micah and I prayed for obvious clarity of direction. My doctor came to see me early last week and had contacted The Fetal Care Center in Cincinnati as well as the Neonatology department here at this hospital. It was clear to him that we go ahead and set a date for delivery for February 13 and we were comfortable with that timing. Apparently, babies diagnosed with TTTS are at much higher risk for things going wrong in-utero versus being born premature at 32 weeks gestation... So there was the light at the end of the tunnel (no pun intended) and I geared up for 9 more days of bed rest. JIOJ ~ February 5, 2012

CHAPTER 15

I had been in the hospital for one week. It was just enough time for me to know what food was the least hospital-y on the menu, become acquainted with all the TV channels, and establish a "stuff" drawer next to the bed. I also had gotten to know many of the staff in and around the unit. The gal that came in to mop and clean was a delightful person. She did her job with intention and calmness. Then there were the nurses. Being a nurse is a difficult job. I remember way back when I was in nursing school, it was clear to me that the lives of the patients in the hospital many times lie in the hands of these persevering, capable, knowledgeable persons who did not call the shots, but gave the shots. There was not anyone else in the ante-partum unit with multiples at the time. There were whispers of other mothers with pre-term labor and preeclampsia around me. Of course, I never had the pleasure of meeting the ladies who were opposite the walls of my room.

I was still determined to be as educated as possible as a lay-medical-person simultaneously growing three babies. I would mentally file every piece of info I gathered from the tests and sonograms, doctor's visits and nurse rounds to help me stay on top of how everyone was doing. There were doctors who came in who were on call for my doctor. I would put them immediately through various tests to get a feel for their understanding of what I was doing in this place and what the goals were. It was a bit of a conundrum. They wanted me carry babies as long as I could and, of course, I wanted to also. Nevertheless, you go and read the statistics about TTTS and its volatile, precarious nature thrust on the living babies in my womb and tell me you would not be conflicted. I really wanted professionals who could make very educated decisions, given all the factors there were to consider.

The good news was that each doc seemed to show me respect. I knew the terminology, I knew my babies, and I had a singular focus. I would do whatever I could to take care of Isaac, Eliana, and Isabella. They would say, "We want to keep you here as long as we can!"

I would say, "Absolutely! As long my babies have three visible bladders, no hydrops, adequate amniotic fluid, and strong doppler readings." Then, they would agree.

Each day I was monitored three times — morning, early afternoon, and evening — for around an hour. Each baby would have a heart monitor and I would have a monitor that measured any uterine contractions. That was quite an ordeal. It is not like each baby was lined up perfectly, bearing his or her heart-side to the flat space of the transducer. I remember at one point, having those round, plastic things propped with washcloths and lying in some crazy uncomfortable position, trying not to move so the nurse could get a steady stream of values to record for that session.

My doc, being the proactive kind, scheduled a visit with one of the neonatologists who served the NICU just upstairs. He was articulate and kind in the way he communicated information, giving Micah and me clarity about what we could be facing with each baby, given his or her gestational age. Receiving the information was helpful and concerning all at the same time. It is an interesting age in which we live, when babies born so early in their development can be helped so much by medication, plastic, metal, imaging technology, and even added calories in the form of powdered formula.

I remember reading about preemies born in the early 1900s who were fed rye whiskey and kept in dresser drawers. I also recall the history of the incubator highlighting a sideshow at Coney Island where folks would pay to see the tiny babies. We are well past that era now, with babies surviving as early as twenty-four weeks gestation. My appreciation for the doctors and nurses dedicated to caring for these infants with such tiny veins and tiny cries, yet enormous needs grew immensely during the weeks we leaned on them so much. There was no better place for me to be, knowing a few floors above me was a Level 4 NICU with staff prepared to care for my babies.

The sixth day of my stay, I had one particular nurse who got very flustered in the whole monitoring process. She would try and hide her frustration, but I could feel it. I would try and help. I almost always knew around the place to find heartbeats as I felt everyone moving in their own, unique ways. With all the sonograms I had, I could usually very easily help the nurses track everyone down. This particular day, frustration was growing. The next morning after the shift change, I was so thankful there was a new nurse and with her a new opportunity to check and make sure each baby was doing okay. However, I was also feeling distress not having had the assurance of a capable, or at least patient, nurse the day before.

It was exactly one week from my admit day, on a Friday. This nurse had a demeanor and confidence that proved a welcomed change from the one prior. She was calm, patient and made sure she got readings on all the babies. I needed her and God had provided her, for a moment such as this.

She found Isaac's heart rate with no problem as well as Isabella's. Then, we began looking for Eliana's. The way she was positioned made her difficult to track down, especially with two larger babies with larger hearts on either side of her smaller body. After a few minutes, my nurse did find her but had to sit and hold the monitor at an angle so she could get an accurate, consistent reading. Eliana was more still than usual but her heart rate was normal — at first. Then, we heard a very audible deceleration. It was not a good sound, like time slowing down, but I knew time was not the issue. The nurse and I looked at each other, then she very calmly started calling for help. The recording device had not picked up the deceleration, but she and I knew exactly what we had heard. I called Micah and asked him to leave work. Within minutes, I had an ultrasound and all appeared to be fine. In the meantime, our doctor was called in and came to sit with us and watch her some more.

Dr. Koontz was not on call that day. He was not even working, if I remember correctly, but he was in the building. His wife was out of town and he had preferred to spend his free time at the hospital. I had asked the physician on call if he would reach him. After he agreed, there was no question or hesitancy in Dr. Koontz's reply. He was there to help, day off or not. He came into my room, sat down calmly, and watched the monitor. We spoke about what was happening. I was in a near panic, knowing that one of my children was in distress. I could not imagine trying to rest knowing what I had seen and heard on the monitor. He agreed, and thankfully he had a plan. As we sat in quiet, giving thought to that plan, Eliana's heart rate dipped again. It was visible on the monitor this time. I will never forget the way it felt to have my doctor say the words to me, "You know what you are asking me to do, don't you?" The implications of delivering babies at thirty-one weeks bear a certain solemnity. All the preparation and prayer, waiting and watching three babies in-utero, ended here.

Within minutes, I was being prepped for surgery. We were moved to a room at the very end of the Labor and Delivery triage department. With monitors everywhere and in a mess of emotions, Micah and I waited to meet our babies. Oh yeah... and I had gone into active labor. As I watched the line rise, sustain, and fall on the monitor that mirrored my contractions, it was clear people were on their way out one way or another. Regardless of my body's obvious readiness to deliver, a C-section was what our doc had felt the best means to bring these little ones out into the world.

I will never forget the sight of the OR. There were three little assessment beds for each of the babies with their names already on them on one whole side of the room. Within minutes, each baby had at least one if not two nurses in ready position to receive them. There was also a neonatologist and a nurse practitioner to oversee the babies' immediate care. They were so eager to get their hands on our babies! The smiles in their eyes above their masks made me feel so much at ease. There were also seven taking care of me — nurses, my perinatologist, an assisting OB/GYN from his same practice, an anesthesiologist and a scrub nurse. There were so many people in that room! I knew there would be a crowd, but seeing everyone filling up almost every space was overwhelming! Micah came in to join us and within minutes Isaac was out. Somehow, he had managed to get a knot in his umbilical cord, which could have presented a huge problem for him. Micah got a picture and was then inspired to take more over-the-curtain pictures (which shall never be seen — rest assured). I now can say I know what my own liver looks like — ugh. Isaac was whisked away to his station. One minute later, Eliana was out. She had the tiniest cry, but she was surely spirited. Another minute later, Isabella was out. She was the first baby I saw, as her bed was parallel to mine. Micah was running around trying to get pictures before the train of babies left the OR. I got to give Isabella a kiss, then she and the others (1st–Eliana, 2nd–Isabella, 3rd–Isaac) made their way up to the NICU. Later, I was told that Andrew and Elijah did get to see their brother and sisters as they were wheeled down the hallway. I was so glad they got a glimpse of them. Back in the OR, my doctor leaned over the curtain and reaffirmed our decision to take them out. He finished the procedure and sent me to recovery.

It wasn't until 4:30 a.m. that I got to see the babies. By that time, they were settled in to their own special spots in the NICU. Later that morning, the big boys left for North Carolina and will be cared for there by family. It was hard to see them leave but reassuring knowing that they will be loved on while Micah and I learn how to navigate the NICU. Already I feel stretched between five children. I knew it was coming, but experience is usually different than I expected and will be a true educator. JIOJ ~ Feb. 5, 2012

There were a few minutes in the recovery room when I remember a meeting with the neonatologist on call that evening. He had assessed each baby and had a positive report for each one. I do not remember much after that, until I woke up around 4 a.m. and immediately wanted to see my babies. I had only a glance at each of them before we parted in the OR. I was so excited to see them and study their little features. I knew they would not look like my boys, since they came with their own, outside-of-me DNA.

Micah helped me into a wheelchair and ushered me into the Neonatal Intensive Care Unit. He had already been once after their births to check on them while I slept, drowsy from anesthesia, and knew just where to go. Their three isolettes were in a line next to the nurses' station in the back corner of the unit. Isaac first, Eliana next, then Isabella: A, B, C, 1, 2, 3. I peeked in on each of them. Those first glances of these babies, first created in 2008, now birthed into our family, were overwhelming to say the least.

Soon after delivery, Isaac had to be placed on a ventilator. His 3 lb. 11 oz. frame was difficult to see as he was tucked and swaddled inside his bed. He was sleeping, propped up, with tubing and tape covering so much of his little face. He looked so small. Then, I turned to Eliana. The 2 lb., 4 oz. little-bittle needed no assistance in her breathing at all. She was stretched out and snoozing as well. Isabella shared the same birth weight as Isaac and was receiving some oxygen therapy. She was sprawled out in a way that proved she was the adventurously flexible one who had been pressing against my lungs and ribcage for the many weeks before. They all had various lines and monitors, and they were alive.

They looked nothing like I had imagined, but more beautiful than I had ever dreamed.

Learning to navigate the NICU came with its share of hardships, too. Neither Isaac, Eliana, nor Isabella had some of the more serious problems many preemies face. It is a solemn place. Within the gathering of world's tiniest inhabitants, intense vulnerability makes itself known even in the environment. In many ways, the tiny ones are the strongest of us.

There are many memorable moments we all shared in the quiet spaces of the NICU. There was the first time I held each baby — the first baths and the first feedings, the first prayers and blessings whispered in the stillness of the evenings I had to leave them.

Isaac came off of the ventilator within a couple of days. He was my last baby to hold. His little blond-red hair brushed against my cheek as he and I nestled into a recliner next to his isolette. "My Shepherd Will Supply My Need" was the song I sang to him in-utero and was the first song I sang to him in our first moments. After having him so inaccessible, it felt so good to physically comfort him.

Eliana needed some extra time. After two weeks without any breathing assistance, her body began to tire. She required a blood transfusion and supplemental oxygen to allow her the rest she needed to grow until she could handle the demands of life out in the world.

Isabella moved her way the fastest through the unit. She did not need supplemental oxygen very long. She was holding her body temperature, gaining weight, and doing all the things full-term babies do within three weeks. From her first moments until today, she is a most content child, easy-going and indeed a beautiful joy.

At three weeks old, Isabella was released and we brought her home. Two days later, Isaac joined her. Two weeks after the homecomings of Isabella and Isaac, and at five weeks old, Eliana joined us all.

CHAPTER 16

This is not a story about a girl who figured it all out and then God gave her what she wanted. This is the continuing story of the One True God, the God of history, pursuing one of His daughters in love, directing her face to His mercy, love, and grace with compassion. In the process, I was allowed to see what love can do for those frozen and waiting. It is a humbling and beautiful thing, mysterious and miraculous.

This season of life, permeated with such a complex mix of joy and suffering, was life changing. Confronted by the law of God, I found my identity in question as I found myself to be a worse sinner than I had known. It made me question eternal realities.

What I was asking myself in the midst of such realizations was, "Are God and I okay?" Why should I ask such a question? As a person who had grown up in church and first believed the Gospel, the law of God had grown to be far more pervasive than I had previously realized. Even through years of knowing about God, I had not found it safe to be known by God. There are Christian words that seem to clean up some things, and I had been good at using them. It always felt too vulnerable, because if I admit that He knows me, then He must know all. All those laws I have been talking about? I know the ones I keep and the ones I do not, as God makes good on His promise to write them on my heart. I realize that I fail and I fail often. I know better, yet I do not always do better. I may or may not have made right choices with right heart attitudes. I certainly did not act perfectly at all times. Even my most noble choices were tainted with sin. When I was so angry and broken, moving down a path of suffering, I could not help but wonder if God was angry with me for failing.

One man, Job, experienced profound suffering. In the midst of it, Job's friends began questioning, and I followed suit. It makes sense, since the world around me functions in and through cause and effect and reciprocation, and success hinges on initiative. However, my own questions and answers did not comfort. Regardless, I am not the judge or justifier of myself. God does divide truth and judge rightly. My own self-estimations do not suffice to hold me secure in His love, and experiencing such profound suffering had amplified the implications of this truth. Suffering tests the most important truths and calls into question ultimate realities.

"Our point of pain reveals to us our greatest need — our need to be set free from false hopes and to cling to the only hope of the gospel."[11] I did not have all the answers, but Good News! They exist outside of me, and suffering brought me to them. The answer to my first question found its roots in the Good News of the Gospel.

To hear good news, we must first hear bad news. For the believer, the bad news keeps getting worse. Through the years as God's Word had infiltrated my life, invading new space, I realized just how desperate I was, like the orphans I longed to love. The admonitions in the Bible do inform actions, attitudes, and motivations. I realized my brokenness, frailty, and dependence, like the little ones I was so driven to remember. The desperation is real.

God is holy. The Old Testament is full of God going to extraordinary means to establish His holiness. He is I AM. He is perfect. He hid Moses

---

[11] Tullian Tchivijian, *Glorious Ruin* (David C Cook, 2012), 159.

in the cleft of the rock and only allowed him to see the tail end of His glory as He passed by, lest he perish[12]. He judges swiftly. Lot's wife was left a pillar of salt[13] and Uzzah killed instantly for steadying the ark of the covenant[14], both examples of disobedience. The people of God wandered in the wilderness for forty years[15]. Even Moses did not make it into the Promised Land[16]. Regardless of my sympathetic response to each of these persons, I know I must not take obedience lightly.

By the teaching ministry of Jesus recorded in the New Testament, commandments etched in stone like, "Do not murder," are brought to censure anger with a brother[17]. Then, there is the non-negotiable, just in case I think I can still live up to the law, "Be perfect as your Father in heaven is perfect."[18] The book of Romans puts it concisely, saying, "All have sinned and fall short of the glory of God." The law of God condemns. It condemns me. It condemns me to death[19]. My sin condemns me to death.

Both the Mosaic Law as well as the laws expressed beyond Mount Sinai describe who God is in His utter perfection and the demands He has on me. The Bible is not a book of things for me to do. It is a book that describes all that I do not do and why I need Jesus to do it all. Romans also says the law came to increase the trespass. Much smarter people than me call this appropriation a use of the law, and it makes sense. The Bible does read me. It explains the perfect plan, the story of the world, and how different I am,

---

[12] Exodus 33:22

[13] Genesis 19:26

[14] 2 Samuel 6:7

[15] Numbers 32:13

[16] Deuteronomy 32:48-52; 34:5

[17] Matthew 5:21-22

[18] Matthew 5:48

[19] Romans 6:23

post-Genesis 3, from the Creator and Law-Maker and the ways I deviate from His plan.

The deviation from the law is sin. Sin separates humanity from God, just as orphans are separated from their birth families. If I want to live eternally with God, or be near Him for even a moment, I need to be different than I am in my natural, born in sin state. I need to be justified, or made right with a Holy God.

The Bible shows over and over again just how lofty a prospect true obedience is — literally. I cannot pay the penalty for sin with good behavior or penance. It does not work that way. Reciprocation is always met with condemnation in regard to the Divine versus the human. I might have known this when I first believed, but how am I to know how God feels about me as the law continues to convict? Even though I am no longer held to the law as a means to gain right-ness with God as a believer, I still know when I transgress, or go beyond it. In fact, I seem to be more and more aware of how often it happens.

James Montgomery Boice writes in his commentary on Romans, when speaking particularly of those being close to the edge of despair over this awareness, "The struggle actually grows stronger rather than weaker..." and that "although the struggle is a real one and difficult, the outcome is not bleak or uncertain but glorious — because of God."[20]

I should not go to more law for life. The book of Galatians argues that hearing with faith by the Spirit both begins the saving work of God and completes it[21]. Later in chapter 3, Paul writes, "Is the law then contrary to the promises of God? Certainly not! For if a law had been given that could give life, then righteousness would indeed be by the law. But the Scripture

---

[20] Boice, *An Expositional Commentary, Romans vol. 2,* 772.

[21] Galatians 3:1-6

imprisoned everything under sin, so that the promise by faith in Jesus Christ might be given to those who believe."

At the point I was trampled by the pain and heartache of losing my babies, feeling as far from the goodness of God I have ever felt, no word of law or descriptions of the triumphant Christian life lifted my head from peering behind the shroud of death. After years of suffering in miscarriage, infertility, and secondary infertility, and when my first adopted babies moved from suspension to eternity, admonitions became burdensome. When statistics and prognosis were bleak, it was not the command to find joy that gave me the strength to move. Simmering in suffering was most effective in stripping away any hope of finding any other way but through Jesus. In and through this most unique and arduous season, it was almost as if I was hearing the Good News for the first time. It was light in darkness, life in death. I did not have anything to add — I knew it to be exactly what it is; a gift of grace alone by faith alone. I needed it when I first believed, and I continued (and continue) to need it after.

The narrative of the whole Bible does not end with the description of those in need. It continues to show us how the "law-maker became the law-keeper and died for us, law-breakers."[22] My suffering and sin were not met with condemnation, but another invitation to repent and believe.

Justification

There are many versions of this question, but the one I found myself asking was, "Are God and I okay?" Another way to say it might be, "Is God eternally displeased with me?" or another, "Have I irreparably damaged our relationship?" The answer is summed up appropriately in Romans 5.

---

[22] Tullian Tchividjian with Nick Lannon, *It Is Finished* (David C Cook, 2015), January 14.

This verse in particular describes those for whom Christ died. The scripture reads, "Therefore, since we have been justified by faith, we have peace with God through our Lord Jesus Christ.[23]" Faith is a gift of God, given through grace[24]. It is by faith that I receive justification[25]. Justification describes me, as one who has believed, like I enter a courtroom where God is judge and Jesus stands trial for me. My past, present, and future sins are many and I know the accusations well[26], but they are inadmissible. In fact, God seems to have forgotten them[27]. Jesus' perfect life is imputed, or attributed, to me. I am declared righteous based on the righteousness of Jesus and the perfect life He lived in my place. All God's anger and wrath against me for the wrongs I have done — past, present, and future sins — have been paid for by Jesus[28]. Not a drop of blood has been neglected or spilled in vain. That was Good News when I first believed, and it continues to be really good news when I am faced with learning I am more sinful than I thought. Justification describes me, just as if I never sinned, just as if I always obeyed. In the end, I have peace with God based on Christ's righteousness, and my soul has peace.

Thanks be to God through Jesus Christ our Lord!

This is why this important phrase is sandwiched between the most brave, self-aware confession in Romans 7. It does not read, "This is really bad! I have to get my act together!" The focus moves to Jesus, because He is the only hope for sinners[29]. Religion describes people doing something to earn

---

[23] Romans 5:1

[24] Eph. 2:8

[25] Romans 3:21-26; 8:30

[26] Hebrews 10:16

[27] Hebrews 8:12; 10:17

[28] Romans 3:25

[29] John 14:6

favor with God. Christians defer to Jesus as the only one Who has earned favor with God. Peace is brought through His work, not mine.

The words of scripture that bring peace, or Good News, are distinct and different than words of law. The Gospel of Grace is singularly good news. Sure, law enlightens, but its effect only reaches so far and serves particular purposes. In contrast, words of Gospel breathe life where there is death. The lack of differentiation explains why it had ceased to be good news that proved life-giving in the face of death, even and especially in the face of suffering. I had bound up the Gospel with law. There are people who have written and taught about law and Gospel (especially justification) in much better and clearer ways than I am able. Those expositions have been so helpful.

In the light of law, I realize my need for more than ways to avoid idolatry. In this life, I cannot rid myself of it! The truth is, I am often convicted of idolatry, but the answer to my idolatry is not more rules to escape it, rather in repentance in hearing again the Word of Hope, the Gospel. Jesus never committed idolatry, but always found perfect satisfaction in His Father alone for me. He lived every day on this earth never substituting His love for His Father for any lesser thing. When my Christian, Holy Spirit awareness shows me to be a law-breaker, I need to be reminded over and over again that Jesus is the only Law-Keeper. Not only did He live a life free from idolatry, He paid the penalty for my sin of idolatry.

The same can be said for distrust, unrighteous anger, and other things I would hope do not constitute my character yet do not evade me. Even though my life is a struggle with sins in various forms, my life is hidden with Christ in God[30]. God's provision for me in Christ Jesus undercuts every space the law invades and advises.

---

[30] Col. 3:3

I need Jesus, who lived a perfect life, always fully obeying every command to the glory of God the Father, to be my substitute. I need Someone who never sinned. When the law condemns actions, attitudes, and all that lies between, I need safety before a Holy God who requires that those who are near Him be like Him. I need Someone to both live a perfect life in all ways in my place and pay the penalty for my sin. This is distinctively Christian.

In matters of faith and the exercise of putting hope in the unseen things of God, whether my ability seems great or small does not ultimately matter. It is perfected, not by what I may or may not muster, but in the Savior Who always demonstrated faith fully, wholly, even to the point of death. The way this works out in the hearts of those Jesus brings to the Father is a mystery. Even while mysterious, it is indeed sure.

As a long-time believer in Jesus Christ, I realized how relevant the Gospel (and particularly justification) is for every day, not just for back when God first saved me. The Gospel is the lifeline to those in Christ. It must not be neglected as life and law call out the unredeemed parts of me as I vacillate between pride and despair, even in my attempts to be obedient. The more I am confronted through the Holy Spirit with the neediness of my soul, the more I need to hear Good News. I needed it when I first believed, and I need it every day. I need it every hour.

The Gospel is for every day. I cannot get over it and move on in becoming more like Jesus. It is my hope in becoming like Jesus. If I get to the point that I believe I have gotten it, that is the day I need it most. The Gospel described in the Bible takes hold of me — it seeks me out every day and puts before me truths too wonderful to fully comprehend. I do not have to be afraid as it reaches into the dark places of my soul.

These truths make Jesus's death for sinners, taking on the full wrath of God for those who repent and believe, seem increasingly remarkable and His resurrection, a true hope for those dying. It solidifies His claim to be "The way, the truth, and the life."

CHAPTER 17

Adoption

I t gets even better. God's love extends beyond making Him and I okay with one another. The way this is accomplished begins to give me a way to answer my second big question: "Where is God in the midst of pain, when all feels like it is falling apart?" or more broadly, "How does God speak into suffering?"

I didn't only need a justifier in the darkest time of my life. I needed to be loved in a tender and merciful way. I needed the One in control of all things to see me hurting and do something about it, much like a child looks to his or her parent for help and consolation. The way this is accomplished then expounded upon is what causes me to marvel at this story. His provision for me does not end in salvation. God provides tender mercy, fulfilled in adoption. I could have never orchestrated such profound irony.

Returning to the courtroom after one has been found righteous based on the life and death of Jesus, God the Judge leaves the bench and approaches the once accused. He invites me into His house and into His family. Not only am I now justified, I have a name. I have a place. I have an inheritance. I have all the benefits of being loved as a daughter, just as in an adoption.

In his book Knowing God, J.I. Packer has this to say:

> *...adoption (is that it) is the highest privilege that the gospel offers: higher even than justification. This may cause raising of eyebrows, for justification is the gift of God on which since Luther evangelicals have laid the greatest stress, and we are accustomed to say, almost without thinking, that free justification is God's supreme blessing to us sinners. None the less, careful thought will show the truth of the statement we have just made.*

> *That justification... is the primary and fundamental blessing of the gospel is not in question. Justification is the primary blessing, because it meets our primary spiritual need. ...*

> *But this is not to say that justification is the highest blessing of the gospel. Adoption is higher, because of the richer relationship with God that it involves. ...Adoption is a family idea, conceived in terms of love, and viewing God as father. In adoption, God takes us into His family and fellowship, and establishes us as His children and heirs. Closeness, affection, and generosity are at the heart of the relationship. To be right with God the judge is a great thing, but to be loved and cared for by God the father is greater. (pp. 186-188)*

God teaches me in the law that He is holy, perfect, and righteous, and I am not. I deserve death for what I have done and left undone. God says to me in the Gospel that Jesus has fulfilled the law's demands for me. Then God communicates to me in adoption that I may now come and be His daughter, abide in Him, and live forever as His child. Learning about law deepens my understanding of the Gospel. Learning about adoption deepens my understanding of the affection of my Father. There is no way I can even consider the tenderness of God except for the justification of my soul provided in Christ. There is no adoption without justification. However, adoption speaks to the degree with which the Father longs to care for His children, not only securing them but doing so in perfect love.

I would not be aware of any of this without the gift of the Holy Spirit.

I found, and still find, my voice echoing Paul as He continues through his writing in the book of Romans. In chapter 8, there are phrases nestled within rich theological teaching that show a response to the tension between human experience and rich truth. The phrase Paul cries after, "O wretched man that I am!" in Romans 7:24 is, "Abba! Father!" Within the context of the passage, the relationship moves from God and sinner, to God and saint, then to Parent and child. "For you did not receive the spirit of slavery to fall back into fear, but you have received the Spirit of adoption as sons… The Spirit himself bears witness with our spirit that we are children of God." The Spirit I received at my conversion has different functions, and one is to testify that I am a child of God.

The book of Galatians is consistent as the Spirit's cry within my heart beckons my Father, declaring I am no longer a slave under the law, but a daughter and an heir through God[31]. He seals those who believe and offers guarantee of my inheritance[32]. God continues to set before me hope of what will be as one who shares the benefits of God the Son.

---

[31] Galatians 4:6-7

[32] Eph. 1:13-14

In the meantime, the Spirit's functions do not end there. The same Spirit comforts and consoles when my groanings are too deep for words[33]. He whispers to our souls in a way human utterances cannot. God goes to great lengths to comfort His people[34].

Since Jesus has bridged the chasm between the law and love, I no longer have God the Judge to fear, but instead have the love of a Father. When sin was revealed and I was suffering, my Father did not say, "You have been a Christian for a long time and you know better." Instead, His disposition toward me in Christ communicates that I am His girl. He kissed my desperate, tear stained face with grace and with the hope of what is to come. He did so in a way that acknowledged the depth of pain this side of heaven and promised to, one day, make it all better. He was proud of me, not in weighing how obedient or trusting I had or had not been, but because of the perfect obedience of His Son, Jesus Christ. In the power of His resurrection, He reminded me that one day my hurt would be replaced with delight. A world of death will be replaced with an eternity of a fully redeemed life. I was no more loved for my obedience or less loved because of my sinfulness. I am loved because God is love, and He loves me.

When He first began my adoption, He did with the knowledge that I would spend my entire earthly life sinning against Him. He knew that by His gift of grace I would believe, yet battle fully believing all the things He says in His word are true. If I believed perfectly, I would act perfectly. God is patient as my flesh battles to try and find my identity in every other place, rather than in the place where I am fully known, loved, named, and secure.

---

[33] Romans 8:26

[34] Ian Smith, *Gospel Transformation Bible* (Crossway, 2013), ed. Bryan Chapell and Dane Ortlund, Galatians 4:1-7 Commentary, 1578-79.

God proved His love for me as my Father. He did not do it in giving me five beautiful children to hold and eight to anticipate holding, already waiting for me with Him. He did it by reminding me that I am His child. He proved it, not in the moment I would evaluate myself at my best, but when I was at my very worst. When my soul cried out in pain and in shame, He met me with the gentleness of Fatherly affection. God gave me a lesson in my identity, not in the things I had done — especially in and through all the events that led up to the adoption of our little ones — but by reminding me of all He has done in my own justification and adoption.

Getting from Already, Not Yet to Eternity: Experiencing Death as the New Living

> *God's love for you is fierce, self-afflicting, white-hot, life-transforming. The goal of this love is that you may be called God's daughter, God's son. All this pain and grief is bent in on one primary goal: your adoption and his eventual praise. Your relationship with the Creator of all there is has been secured in the blood and tears of love's delight. Your Father is no longer far off, no longer a stranger, no longer a judge. Now he's your Father. John wants us to see that we are called God's children because we are his children, even now.*[35]

What is continually intriguing about justification and adoption is the already, not yet aspect of the benefits that extend to those God loves. The apostle Paul uses this language often in descriptions of what is realized and what is true outside our limited understanding.

---

[35] Elyse M. Fitzpatrick, *Comforts from the Cross* (Crossway, 2009), 76-77.

One of the most beautiful and explicit scriptures expounding God's adoptive love is 1 John 3:1-3: "See what kind of love the Father has given to us that we should be called children of God; and so we are. The reason why the world does not know us is that it did not know him. Behold, we are God's children now, and what we will be has not yet appeared; but we know that when he appears we shall be like him, because we shall see him as he is. And everyone who thus hopes in him purifies himself as he is pure."

There are many Christians who preach and write about sanctification, or the process by which those who believe are made like Jesus. One thing I am sure of: In the lives of those God loves as sons and daughters, sanctification is a promise[36]. It may or may not come with my complete understanding and participation. I may try to give it its own clothing or paint it on myself with systems of disciplines and even good works, but regardless of the form, if change has occurred, it has come through death. In this space between what is true and what is fully realized, a large part of purification comes through encountering the law of God and experiencing, again, the Gospel. This process causes me to die to all the unredeemed parts of me that look for hope outside the Good News. The Christian life is no longer about living for God; it is about dying, cross-carrying. Death is the backdrop to this world, this side of eternity. Even my best efforts to love had been met with death. It is the appointment we all share that reminds us to look for hope elsewhere, outside this world.

Purification and new life follows death to one's old self. No one signs up for death, especially death to oneself. Self-preservation is in my God-given biology. Spiritual self-preservation most usually shows up in me as anything that disallows awareness of my utter need and dependence on God for absolutely everything. I experience death when I look for

---

[36] John 17:17; Heb. 9:13-14; 1 Thess. 5:23-24

salvation in any place other than in the justification bought for me by the perfect life and atoning death of Jesus. It enters in to every part of my flesh that tries to look for an identity outside the one given to me in Christ. It reaches in to any hope beyond the grave that was not secured in the resurrection of Christ. Death will continue until I shed this shell completely.

It is a painful process. There has to be death for the deepening, underpinning of truths too wonderful for me to imagine on my own. My old self, still living in light of Romans 7, constantly vacillates between pride and despair in failure and obedience. There are changes that may be observed on the outside, but I dare not diminish the law to make me feel okay. The more I focus on me and how I am doing, the more I struggle. The more I focus on Jesus and what He has done, the more hope I have as I cling to the promise that I am being made like Him by His own work and in the promise of 1 John.

Sanctification by the Spirit always points me outward, outside of me. Being reminded that there is constantly and consistently Good News beyond my circumstances is paramount. I am thankful God provides the means for remembrance each week in the preaching of His Word, the Lord's Supper, and through the ministry of His church. I am very thankful for friends who remind me and hold truth out when I am weak. There are many who come to mind immediately as they play parts in this story. When I forgot or found my flesh failing, their voices, either by word or deed, held out truth.

God has not chosen to make me like Him now. As John says, "But we know that when he appears we shall be like him, because we shall see him as he is."

John Newton speaks so insightfully about our experience between conversion and the appearing of the Savior. Barbara Duguid has written an excellent book recounting his thoughts on these things. She says, "God could have saved us and made us instantly perfect. Instead, he chose to save us and leave indwelling sin in our hearts and bodies to wage war against the new and blossoming desires to please God that accompany salvation."[37]

The space between what God demands and what I actually do in this time before He appears evidences unbelief. Unbelief manifests itself in sin. If I really, truly believed, I would fully obey all the time, but I do not. There is sin in everything here within the confines of humanity, even in my good works. In these spaces, I am continually reacquainted with the man in Mark. This leads me to repeatedly to pray, "Lord I believe, help my unbelief." Jesus does and will.

Yet in all circumstances, belief rests in the perfection of Jesus, the object of my faith. My identity is secure in His finished work on my behalf. I am safe to struggle, to repent and believe, continually given opportunities to realize I am far more sinful than I imagined but I am far more loved than I ever dared hope.[38]

The means by which I continue to see and experience the depth of my known depravity continues to be my biggest suffering. What could be more sanctifying than learning day by day, minute by minute, that I am more sinful than I thought, yet I am loved more deeply than I can imagine? Allowing the law to be what it is, implicating and convicting, maintains the purity and beauty of the Gospel. The promises of God in justification and adoption make it safe to continue to live in this way. My sins — past, present, and future — have been nailed to the cross and I bear them no more.

Suffering here is real. It bears witness to the brokenness of this world. It speaks to the weight of redemption promised. This is important to

[37] Barbara R. Duguid, *Extravagant Grace* (P&R Publishing, 2013), 30.

[38] Jack Miller, Reference unknown.

consider as I am called to weep with those who weep. I think especially of my friends and neighbors who are suffering from all kinds of pain. Real pain, pain that Jesus came to address in overcoming the world[39], is not something I need to dismiss or diminish for the sake of proving Christianity or the goodness of God. The life we see and now experience heralds the time of salvation, but it is not the time of redemption. Dying hurts. Losing babies hurts. Infertility hurts. God is sympathetic to us in our weaknesses. He does not demand that I deny the hurt, but wants me to embrace it as something fallen that He will make beautiful in due time. I also have the benefits of Christ, my Savior and Brother, who lived on earth and experienced pain and death and, as my High Priest, sympathizes with my weaknesses[40]. He always lives to intercede for me[41], sitting at the right hand of God.

This age before redemption is a complex mix of joy and pain. Even as I embrace both realities, I still reach out for the hem of the garment of the Healer. Sometimes, heaven breaks through and I am given a clear vision of Divine intervention. Sometimes God writes new histories that defy my limited logic, and sometimes He does not. The author of the words from 1 John also penned the book of Revelation. John the apostle saw a world beyond this one where there will be no more sometimes. All the moments that display the workings of God bent on redeeming a broken world point to this day. Sally Lloyd-Jones paraphrases John's words in the Jesus Storybook Bible. I love this book. It is beautiful. Among the events John records are these words reflecting the end of the adoption process.

---

[39] John 16:33

[40] Hebrews 4:15

[41] Hebrews 7:25

And the King says, "Look!
God and his children are together again.
No more running away. Or hiding.
No more crying or being lonely or afraid.
No more sick or dying.
Because all those things are gone.
Yes, they're gone forever.
Everything sad has come untrue.
And see—I have wiped away every tear from every eye![42]

The Gospel along with the promises of God, both in justification and adoption, remain a humbling mystery. I do not fully grasp such sacred truths, but by the grace of God, they continue to take hold of me. In effect, the person at the heart of the Gospel takes hold of me. One day, faith will be fully realized and my outer being will match the inner soul that rests secure in a place my eyes have not seen by the work a person I long to be near. One day, the beauty of the promises reserved for those loved by the God of Abraham will be fully known and experienced.

Loving our (Frozen) Neighbors

When I realize that I have been loved with such a great love, it draws me in to love others. It is a natural outworking of understanding the condemnation of the law and the freedom of the Gospel of grace given to sinners. I continually need to hear the Gospel today and every day if I have any hope in loving God and then my neighbors — even my cryo-preserved little ones. The clear, undiluted Gospel inspires love of the self-sacrificing

---

[42] Sally Lloyd-Jones, *The Jesus Storybook Bible* (Zondervan, 2012), 347.

kind. The law is good for helping me see practical ways of showing love to those around me.

For snowflakes, what can be said of each of them — regardless of their infinite differences in structures, shapes, and sizes — are their sustaining environments. Like snowflakes, those who trust Jesus have a sustaining environment; an environment of grace secured for them by their justification and adoption.

Love outside of me has kept pursuing me. Love led me to love orphaned embryos again. When I wanted to run, I did not, and I thank God for that.

I think of how God went after my little ones, frozen in a lab for years, in orchestrating the rescue plan lived out by Micah and me. What an elaborate way to show His faithfulness and resolve to love! What if the call to love orphans teaches more about what God has done for us than what we do for them? When I hear the Gospel, it makes me want to point others toward such a love. I adopted because I have been adopted. I love orphans because I, like them, have been loved.

I pray that many are led to go after these frozen ones. I pray that each one would be cared for in a way that honors God. I also pray that even in the midst of suffering from infertility, we would consider how to continually honor human life as made in the image of God and what that means when negotiating fertility treatments. It also seems appropriate to pray that the church of Jesus Christ would be a safe place for those experiencing these sufferings. When those around us are most vulnerable and suffering, I hope they see within the church a beacon of hope and compassion. God help us make intelligent, thought through plans from the beginning so we are not continuing to add to the numbers of indefinitely frozen persons.

Ultimately, God wants me to know Him as more than a cause to do something good; He wants me to know Him as my Father. He wants to give me something more than children or a reason to write; He wants to give me Himself. All my attempts at loving Him or my neighbors always (and I do not use that word flippantly) point me to His love for me. I pray it spills out in ways that point to Him.

CHAPTER 18

There's a Certain Slant of Light,
Winter Afternoons —
That oppresses, like the Heft
Of Cathedral Tunes —

Heavenly Hurt, it gives us —
We can find no scar,
But internal difference,
Where the Meanings, are —

None may teach it — Any —
'Tis the Seal Despair —
An imperial affliction
Sent us of the Air —

When it comes, the Landscape listens — Shadows — hold
their breath —
When it goes, 'tis like the Distance
On the look of Death —

Emily Dickinson, "There's a Certain Slant of Light" (1861)

I n seventeen years of marriage, Micah and I have only owned three of the eighteen structures we have called home. In all the years and all the spaces, Micah has reminded me again and again that any home here is only a metaphor for our heavenly home. Boy, have we lived that out, whether we have always tried or not!

With life moving in a direction that allows permanence in the foreseeable future without the prospect of leaving, we decided that it was a good time to buy a house again. After weeks of praying and looking, a particular house caught my eye. It seemed a good place with plenty of space to settle for a while and watch our growing children grow.

In the course of a few days, we met with a realtor and mortgage broker and wrestled with what to do. The house had been started, but it was not past the foundation stage. A developer in the area would complete it once a buyer was found. There were so many things that attracted us to it. Micah and I would be able to make it ours and best suit the needs of our not-so-ordinary family. The artist in me would be given an opportunity to emerge and pick all the floorings, wall colors, and lighting. There are clear things that serve a family with unique needs (like lots of little kids) that we could incorporate. One evening before our decision was to be made, we drove by the lot. In planned communities, there are houses in rows with plots for future homes in spaces around them. When we got to the site, the basement had been poured. Micah, Andrew, Elijah, and I walked the exterior and tried to imagine a house sitting there. The boys were really interested in the yard space and were elated that it appeared we were buying a swimming pool, as the rain had collected within the concrete walls. I noticed that on one side, we would be in close proximity to another home, yet to be built. On the other, there was green space.

There were old, tall trees in the open side, waving in the breeze. There was also an overgrown area enclosed by a simple, white, dilapidated fence.

The space just beyond was used as staging for the construction vehicles and materials needed for the homes springing up all around. In other areas, there were piles of rock and dirt — a perfect playground for bigger boys. It was so peaceful that first evening. With confirmation by way of no clear, waving red flags, we left.

At our next meeting with the realtor, we made clear our intention to begin the process of buying this home. We talked again through our part and theirs. I asked about the location of the house, thinking it would be at the end of the road. That was confirmed. Then I happened to mention the green space at the open side of our lot.

"It's a cemetery," the realtor stated.

At first, I was a bit surprised and shocked that a cemetery would sit in the middle of this house-to-house community. It was communicated that this land had a rich history going back to the Revolutionary War. The soil has cradled the inhabitants through many births and deaths.

A few months later, our home was completed. After moving in, I looked into the lives of those whose earthly bodies lie in wait next door. There is a couple, husband and wife, whose gravestones are the most readable. There is a man who was a soldier. There are a few unmarked graves symbolizing several buried from a terrible massacre. There may be a former nun (given the remembrance on the stone). There is also a baby with a completely different last name than any of the others. I have done some research about this little one. One of my theories regarding the reason this child's body rests here alone is that he was a victim of the cholera epidemic. It was not uncommon for babies to be given to orphanages during the outbreak to try and prevent exposure. I have heard stories of an orphanage that was once on this property, so this scenario makes sense. I only speculate. This spot is a physical reminder of so much suffering, through so many years, by those of different ages.

I find it satisfyingly, morbidly ironic that here is where I will hopefully spend many seasons. Some people might cringe at the thought of living so close to such a space that geographically speaks to the finality of this life. For me it is only fitting. This is where I live this side of eternity anyway, in the space between life and death. There will be a day when I will enter a place of complete rest, fully redeemed. No more death. No more sin. That day is not today.

I will not soon forget the Advent Season of 2014. My church invited Ashley Null to speak. His comments were kindly pastoral and stirring, to say the least. He made lengthy reference to the time between our Good Friday and Easter morning. When I feel Good Friday looming, his words remind me that while I may not know when, my Easter Morning is coming. I do not know how long it will be until all will be made new and I will shed this failing skin and the sins that so grieve me.

I do not know the joys and sufferings that lie quietly in the corners of my remaining days here, but in the end the God of Love, the God of the Bible, wins. Easter morning is coming. Hope is secure. I continue to die to my works of false righteousness, led by the law of God. As dismal as that sounds, it is the law that continues to usher me into the Good News of the Gospel each and every day. Those words meet me like a fresh drink of water, a deep breath, and offer peaceful soul-settling. Jesus has justified me. Then again, the heart behind hope belongs to God, my Father, who has adopted me and sealed me with His Spirit. He, being the Author of the story, loves me. Lord, I believe. Help my unbelief.

Until then, I look at my children and see the handiwork of Jesus, as He has helped me believe a little more today than I did yesterday. Their lives are miracles — in this time and in a way I can see. I love that I get a front row seat to watch them grow into who God has made each one of them to be. My husband and I are bonded together in marriage and strengthened in experience. He sees me and continues to call me beautiful, scars and all. Sometimes we talk about the genetic families who chose life and not destruction for our little ones. May God be near to them. Thankfulness is indelibly imbedded in the memories of the days gone by and shapes our future. May the Lord help us remember, lest we forget.

Even as I see and enjoy the smiles of the ones with whom I share my days, I will continue to grieve the children we lost, already with Jesus. I am thankful, yet sober. The same eyes bear tears of elation and wonder, yet weep as I remember the pain of loss.

"Joy will never come by denying our deep sinfulness; rather, it must come by seeing how huge our sin really is and how completely it has been dealt with in Christ."[43] Lasting joy is not lost in momentary awareness of my continued struggle. There is a peace that enters when my eyes focus again on the object of my faith; rather the person, Jesus, who continues to save and intercede. When it happens, if only for a brief second, blessed self-forgetfulness becomes my favorite disposition. The Good News continually seeps in and directs my face to the One taking hold of me.

The creation of my family was indeed a beautiful display of something profound and bigger than those who played the parts. As amazing as the story of my family might be, it pales in comparison to God's work to adopt sinners into His family. My life as a sinner-made-daughter is a miracle. One day, I will thank Him with a completely pure heart. When I have seen His face, I will finally see my eight children gone before me. My aging arms ache to hold them and study each of their faces.

Until then, you may see me stop and stare in kind curiosity at a child bearing their perceived ethnic resemblance, dreaming about what each one may look like.

---

[43] Duguid, *Extravagant Grace*, pg. 99.

There will be a day when faith will be sight. The scene will match that of Psalm 23 on the other side of the valley of the shadow of death; a quiet field and trickling stream with springs of living water, then a table with unending measures of my Father's supply. Every tear will be wiped away, and weeping shall be no more[44]. Pure joy and delight will move in the hearts of those who call Him Father. My little ones gone before me, who have not known a day out of the presence of Jesus, will teach me to sing the songs of heaven. On that day, not before, I will wholly realize the words I have sung to each of my children from the beloved hymn by Isaac Watts ,"My Shepherd Will Supply My Need."

There would I find a settled rest
While others go and come
No more a stranger, nor a guest
but like a child at home.

---

[44] Revelation 7:17

Appendix A

TO THOSE SUFFERING

This is a story about miracles. Yes, it shows God still works today beyond the realm of human understanding. Sometimes He does things in ways we like and have even asked for, but sometimes He does not. I do not know why.

I know there are women who pray daily for the gift of a child to hold. I know there are mommies who have children who have gone on to be with Jesus. I know there are those who have adopted embryos or battled TTTS who will not see the faces of their babies this side of heaven. If you are one of these women, I want you to know that I sit with you in the middle of the whys and heartbreak and wait with you until our Easter morning. I am so sorry for your pain. God is so kind to hear our lament and our questions that communicate, "How long, O Lord?" I ask those questions with you and for you, even when you feel you may have lost your voices. I may, at times, need you to do the same for me.

God has been merciful to me. It was not because I handled everything correctly. Clearly, I would be lying to say that I did. Any degree of faithfulness I have shown illuminates Jesus' faithfulness and my obedience is His. Any prayers met His ears first, and when my words failed He interceded for me. I am so thankful that in all things, He is my substitute. Even more importantly, I pray this story speaks to the love of the Father for His daughter. He loves you with a passion that is relentless and will not cease. I pray wherever you are this love, His love, meets you in the darkness. I pray that by His Spirit, you hear Gospel words in the quiet (and even painfully loud) spaces in your soul and know Him close to you when you feel alone. May we pray together for bolsters of belief and hope in the coming day, when He will wipe the tears from all our eyes.

Appendix B

FOR THOSE WHO STRUGGLE WITH HOW TO HONOR LIFE IN THE MIDST OF INFERTILITY OR SECONDARY INFERTILITY:

I must first say that no matter what, I believe as I have stated: No one is justified by respect for those bearing the image of God nor disqualified for salvation for failing to do so. The prayer of confession found in The Book of Common Prayer speaks to sins done and things left undone. Our hope is in Christ, who always honored life and never diminished or extinguished it. No one perfectly honors those bearing the image of the Triune God except Christ Jesus. For those who trust Him, our lives are hidden with Him in God. His record is ours. He is faithful to receive us in faith and repentance.

As we confess this truth, love moves in and through us toward loving our neighbors, particularly our closest neighbors — our children. We live in an interesting time, when there are so many choices that bear out in ways that do uphold the inherent value of human life, made in the image of God. Some choices are clear, and others less black and white.

If you find yourself suffering through infertility or secondary infertility, I first pray for someone who will walk this road with you with compassion. We all need others to bear with us in ways that minister to us in our hurts. If you find yourself seeking interventions and at the same time desiring to honor the lives of your future children, I am praying for friends, particularly within a body of those confessing the name of Jesus Christ, who will help you navigate such things. If you are looking for other resources that engage these issues, *The Infertility Companion* by Sandra L. Glahn, Th.M. and my friend, the late William R. Cutrer, M.D., *Fearfully and Wonderfully Made: Ethics and the Beginning of Human Life* by Dr. Megan Best, as well as *Embryo: A Defense of Human Life* by Robert P. George and Christopher Tollefsen are books I would generally recommend.

For more information regarding embryo adoption, some resources include the National Embryo Donation Center,[45] Nightlight Christian Adoptions,[46] and various other local reproductive endocrinology clinics providing embryo adoption services. Regardless of where they might be found or how long they have been cryo-preserved, I pray all little ones be remembered and their lives honored.

---

[45] www.embryodonation.org

[46] www.Snowflakes.org | www.Nightlight.org

CPSIA information can be obtained
at www.ICGtesting.com
Printed in the USA
FFOW05n1555080617

9 781498 474030